The Feel of the Work Place

Fritz Steele
Development Research Associates and
Graduate School of Education,
Harvard University

Stephen Jenks
University of New Hampshire

The Feel
of the
Work Place

**Understanding and
Improving Organization Climate**

 Addison-Wesley Publishing Company
Reading, Massachusetts
Menlo Park, California • London • Amsterdam
Don Mills, Ontario • Sydney

Cartoons by Diane Berlew

Past tense

Preface

This book is intended to help people learn something about organization climate: what influences it, what its consequences are, and how it can be changed. By using the metaphor of the weather, we have tried to highlight the kinds of organizational issues that can be identified and explored if we allow ourselves to think freely in metaphorical terms. Many of the concepts and illustrations utilized came from ranging back and forth between physical- and social-climate dynamics, trying to be attuned to their similarities and differences.

Other authors have similarly made use of metaphors — Goffman's choice of the theater as a metaphor for day-to-day social interaction[1] and Berne's game imagery in *Games People Play*[2] are well-known examples. We believe that any person who works in an organization can learn more about that process by creatively manipulating the metaphors that help him or her discover more about what life is like in that organization. Is it a king and his court? A battlefield with unclear boundaries and vague uniforms? A giant marketplace where the vendors and the tourists are all mixed up and you can't tell the players without a program? Depending on the situation and your own style of thinking, any of these images and many others could trigger greater understanding of the dynamics of your organizational life.

We do not, of course, think that organization climate is the only relevant concept for understanding how you live in a sys-

---

[1]Goffman, E., *Presentation of Self in Everyday Life* (Garden City, L.I.: Anchor Books (Doubleday), 1959).
[2]Berne, E., *Games People Play* (New York: Grove Press, 1964).

tem. We chose it because it pulls together a lot of experiences that make up the overall "feel" of a place. Climate is only *one* way of looking at a system and its effects on its members and itself. There are obviously many others: power dynamics, formal structures, friendship patterns, task requirements, learning processes, and so on. We would like the discussion of climate to stimulate the reader into further explorations into the nature of organizational life, from as many different angles as possible. Organizations are created by and for human beings, even if that is sometimes hard to perceive or believe; and if the general level of understanding of organizational dynamics increases, it is our belief that the quality of organizational life can improve as well.

We owe debts to a large number of people who helped us with various stages of the book. We only have space to thank a few of them, including Warner Burke, Clay Alderfer, Deborah Jones-Steele, Jenifer McKinnon, and Dick Hackman.

Finally, we gratefully dedicate this book to the fabulous Squando Palovande, the greatest setter of climate that we have ever known.

September 1976   FS
                                                                   SJ

Contents

Chapter 1

What is Organization Climate?

The concept of organization climate, although alternately accepted and rejected by organization members, management theorists, and behavioral scientists, has nevertheless been used, studied, and talked about for many years. As an explanatory factor, it can serve to show why things are as good or as bad as they are in a particular organization; as a description of the organization itself, it can help to characterize the overall ambience of an organizational system.

This book is written in the belief that, if used properly, climate can indeed be a useful way of thinking about the health of an organization. Unfortunately, as conceptualizations of organization climate have become more elaborate (and more closely tied to the operations used to measure climate, such as questionnaires and factor analyses), the chances of employees actually using the concept have been correspondingly reduced. Organization climate has become a technical term referring to the particular scheme of whichever "expert" happens to be speaking or writing.

Our purpose here is to take the concept of organization climate back to its simpler (and hopefully more useful) interpretations, and thereby provide a means for those who spend their work lives in human organizations to better understand and influence the climate in their particular work group. We hope to stimulate people to think about the climate of their systems, including how they and others are affected by that climate, how they have a part in setting and/or changing the climate, and what alternative climates are open to them.

THE VALUE OF THE CONCEPT OF CLIMATE

In recent years, behavioral scientists and practitioners have taken an increasing interest in an organizational phenomenon called "The Quality of Work Life." Articles are being written about it, consultants are trying to improve it, conferences are focusing on it, and at least one state (Pennsylvania) has commissioned researchers to help improve it in the state's industrial organizations.

Quality of Work Life (or QWL) is usually defined as a technological problem related to the alienating nature of many jobs. In addition, it is generally viewed as primarily a bluecoliar-worker problem, for QWL concerns have been most visible in this segment of the working population. We believe, however, that QWL is an issue relevant to anyone who spends a significant part of his or her waking hours earning a living in an organization.

We also believe that job design is only one cause of QWL problems. Another big contributor is the social climate in which the job is embedded: what it *feels like* to be at work in the system—stresses, demands, pleasures, constraints, opportunities, etc. These aspects form a pattern that constantly exerts subtle but real influences on the worker's life experience. For instance, doing an interesting job in a destructive social climate does not necessarily provide a high-quality work life; it may increase stress by keeping a person in conflict about whether or not to leave the system. This book describes social climate as a factor in the quality of work life, as well as a factor influencing the effectiveness of organizational functioning.

WHAT IS ORGANIZATION CLIMATE?

Recently, climate has often been used as a diagnostic tool, usually to help consultants quickly grasp what a system is like and what it means to the people who inhabit it. The simplest and most useful conceptualization of climate in our work is the literal one: the metaphor of the weather. In this book we will use organization climate to mean *what it feels like to spend time in a social system*—the "weather" in that region of social space. This is basically an experiential definition; that is, it takes its meaning and reality from the experiences and feelings of the people who must work within the social system.

The climate of an organization, then, is the characteristic "weather" in that system or its parts (there may be different climates in different regions of the system). This is basically a property of the system, not just of the persons involved, although they are major contributors to the climate. Whether or not particular people function well in a particular organization climate depends on both the climate and their own feelings, just as it does in different geographic regions. Also, a climate that is good for a person at one stage of his or her development may not be appropriate for a later one—there is not necessarily a continuing good match between people and climates.

It should be emphasized that references to "climate" generally mean the *internal* climate of a system—the characteristics that provide the day-to-day environment for those who work in the system. We mention this because there often is some confusion between internal climate and the climate in which an organization operates—the surrounding environment of the system as a whole, as discussed, for instance, by Lawrence and Lorsch[1]. This surrounding environment has an influence on internal climate, but it is not synonymous with it.

DIMENSIONS FOR ANALYZING THE IMPACT OF CLIMATE

In our work with client systems and our study of others' research on organizational life, a pattern has emerged. The impact of organization climate on members often seems to be similar to the consequences of varying meteorological climates. We have summarized these consequences under four general headings:

(E) how much *total energy* people have available to them;

(D) how the human energy is *distributed or used;*

(P) the extent to which people get *pleasure and enjoyment* from time spent in the organization;

(G) how much people *grow and develop* within the system.

Different climates produce different consequences in the four areas, and it is the mix of consequences which makes the climate feel desirable or undesirable for a particular person. The kinds of organizations and types of people who inhabit different geographical areas are influenced by the prevailing weather patterns, or climate. The same can be said of organizations: the kinds of work groups and types of individuals differ from organization to organization as a consequence of each system's internal climate. These differences become manifest in each of the four dimensions.

(E) Total Energy Available

All of us have experienced the effects different climates can have on our own energy level. Some areas, like the deep South in the summer, can prove almost completely enervating. Writers who have gone to the Caribbean to "work" often report that their plans did not quite pan out—the pace and weather just seemed to encourage a much lower rate of activity than they had intended to maintain.

For a graphic description of low-energy climate, consider Speer's account of life in Hitler's entourage at Obersalzberg:

> To animate these rather barren evenings, sparkling wine was handed around, and after the occupation of France, confiscated champagne of a cheap brand; Goering and his air marshals had appropriated the best brands. From one o'clock on some members of the company, in spite of all their efforts to control themselves, could no longer repress their yawns. But the social occasion dragged on in monotonous, wearing emptiness for another hour or more, until at last Eva Braun had a few words with Hitler and was permitted to go upstairs. Hitler would stand up about a quarter of an hour later, to bid his company goodnight. Those who remained, liberated, often followed those numbing hours with a gay party over champagne and cognac.
>
> In the early hours of the morning we went home dead tired, exhausted from doing nothing. After a few days of this I was seized by what I called at the time "the mountain disease." That is, I felt exhausted and vacant from the constant waste of time.[2]

By contrast, other organizations have climates similar to our Pacific Northwest, or with changes like the seasons in New

England, which stimulate people to activity rather than lulling them into relaxation.

Both kinds of climates have emerged in the organizations and groups we have studied. In fact, many of the common stereotypes of different occupations are based on images we have about the amount of energy available. For example, consider the contrast between our image of the typical banking business and that of the advertising business. Bankers are portrayed as deliberate, slow moving, and cautious, while advertising people are portrayed as energetic, fast paced, and flamboyant.

A variety of internal and external factors can influence the internal climate. Overstaffed systems tend to be less vigorous than lean ones; young organizations tend to be more vigorous than old ones; external competitive pressures can stimulate increased activity; the nature of the market place can affect energy level. Social norms about how much work can be done help to produce systems comparable to the Caribbean, where the pace is slow and people bring a fairly low level of energy to it on a day-to-day basis. The total input level tends to be circumscribed, and this is accepted as natural and normal—simply the way the "world" is. Similarly, there are systems or groups that we could only describe as "hopped-up" or "supercharged" in that everyone seems to put a tremendous amount of energy into the functioning of the system. These systems are not necessarily more productive than systems having a low-energy climate; that depends on the distribution of energy, as we will describe in a moment. But productive or not, certain systems have a high average energy level, and it feels different to be there than it does in a low-energy system. There usually is more stimulation, people make more demands on one another, and time expectations of when something will be done are shorter. There also may be more movement, and more general signs of "busyness."

To get a feel for the differences between low- and high-energy climates, compare these two descriptions of working paces:

Ignoring the chief clerk and myself, they sat down at the far end of the long table, produced more papers from briefcases, and continued their conversation. They were followed in a minute by a youngish lieutenant-colonel, with the air of a don in uniform, who this time muttered a faint 'good morning' in my direction, then joined the sailor and airman in whatever they were discussing. It was impossible to remain unaware of an atmosphere of exceedingly high pressure in this place, something much more concentrated, more intense, than that with which one was normally surrounded.... In this brightly lit dungeon lurked a sense that no one could spare a word, not a syllable, far less a gesture, not of direct value in implementing the matter at hand. The power principle could almost be felt here, humming and vibrating like the drummings of the teleprinter.[3]

And, by contrast:

His life was very regular. He would arrive in the morning just in time to sign his name in the attendance-book before it was removed to the accountant's room. That was at ten o'clock. From ten to eleven he would potter. There was nothing going on at that time in his department, and Mr. Waller seemed to take it for granted that he should stroll off to the Postage Department and talk to Psmith, who had generally some fresh grievance against the ring-wearing Bristow to air. From eleven to half past twelve he would put in a little gentle work. Lunch, unless there was a rush of business or Mr. Waller happened to suffer from a spasm of conscientiousness, could be spun out from half past twelve to two. More work from two till half past three. From half past three till half past four till five either a little more work or more pottering, according to whether there was any work to do or not. It was by no means an unpleasant mode of spending a later January day.[4]

Parts of the same organization may vary widely on the energy dimension. Probably each reader can specify for himself or herself which units tend to feel like the "action" areas of their system and which ones feel like the "Floridas" or "retirement villages," where expectations for input are noticeably less. Sometimes this shows up in the pattern of lunch behavior—how much time is taken for lunch and the nature of prescribed lunch rituals. Other indicators are norms governing speed of work and when projects should be completed.

We have a very energetic colleague who once took a job with a highly successful national company which happened to be a low-energy system. He seemed to be constantly out of step with others and found himself feeling impatient and frustrated most of the time. He tried pouring his energy into his work rather than into trying to change the system, and was told to stop taking work home in the evening—the company felt all work could and should be done during normal working hours. He finally left the organization after deciding that its energy input level and his energy input level were incompatible. His experience illustrates the self-perpetuating nature of low-energy systems. Because high-energy people tend to leave, the system in question will not have a higher rate available to it at periods when it is most important to function more intensively.

What are the contributing factors to low-energy? Group norms against too energetic inputs ("a good member cools it here") may be in effect, as they often are in assembly-line organizations. Management style is another key factor. The whole tone of management may be what Blake and Mouton term "Country Club Management" (the 1, 9 corner of the Managerial Grid): we have our fun, and if we get something done, so much the better.[5] Another factor is the nature of the work and the people's feelings of involvement in it. The less they care about what they or the company is doing, the lower will be their motivation to devote the full capabilities of their energy to events at work, and the more likely they are to put that energy into extraorganizational uses. Similarly, a system in a stable environment doing routine activities may stimulate very little desire to put much energy into work. (Although those environments that do not change are becoming fewer every day.)

What are some major contributing factors to high-energy? Again, group norms against taking it easy may contribute to a great deal of activity—working long hours, working during meals, etc. High energy may be stimulated by feelings of "one-upmanship" or competition within the system: who is the hardest worker; who is the most committed; who is most innovative, etc. An atmosphere of tension or conflict tends to be energizing. Finally, the fact that most organizational systems exist in a rapidly changing environment contributes to the generation of high levels of energy input. A high concern for basic survival tends to energize group members to action.

(D) Distribution of Energy

The second dimension for noting the consequences of climate is the distribution of energy within the system. Given a general level of available energy in the system's people and groups, how does it get used? There are several demands on the available energy in any organizational system, and these demands usually are in competition. Some common energy demands are: short-term productivity versus long-term development; start-up activities versus production activities; survival versus risk-taking; following procedures versus solving problems; etc.

For example, consider the distribution of system energy implicit in Powell's description of a military-records specialist at work:

> His woolly grey hair, short thick body, air of perpetual busy-ness, suggested an industrious gnome conscripted into the service of the army; a gnome who also liked to practice considerable malice against the race of men with whom he mingled, by making as complicated as possible every transaction they had to execute through himself. Diplock was totally encased in military obscurantism. Barker-Shaw, the F.S.O.—as Bithel mentioned, a don in civil life—had cried out in a moment of exasperation, that Diplock, with education behind him, could have taken on the whole of the Civil Service, collectively and individually, in manipulation of red tape; and emerged victorious. He would have out-done them all, Barker-Shaw said, in pedantic observance of regulation for its own sake to the detriment of practical requirement. Diplock's answer to such criticism was always the same: that no other way of handling the matter existed. Filling in forms, rendering 'states', the whole process of documentation, seemed to take the place of religion in his inner life. The skill he possessed in wielding army lore reached a pitch at which he could sabotage, or at least indefinitely protract, almost any matter that might have earned the disapproval of himself or any superior of whom he happened to be the partisan—in practice, Colonel Hog-bourne-Johnson—while at the same time, if something un-usual had to be arranged Diplock always said he knew how to arrange it."[6]

As with the weather, the energy distribution in the system is affected by several factors. The energy necessary to keep a large system running is one factor. The amount of reporting, presenting of projects, and paperwork in many organizations is more than enough to give people the feeling that most of their effort is being put into standing still or running in circles. Another factor determining energy distribution is the organization's system of rewards and sanctions. If rewards can be earned for putting energy into short-term productivity at the expense of longer-term skill development, that is where the energy will be spent. Similarly, if people fear loss of livelihood, esteem, or membership, energy will be expended in image management and/or covering one's tracks.

Classic industrial-psychology studies have often found that under some conditions workers put their time and ingenuity into doing a better job, and under other conditions or climates they put at least as much ingenuity into "beating the system."[7] In the latter case, the climate causes energy to be split among production, managing one's life space, and getting revenge for the feeling of being overcontrolled. (Another way of looking at it from the inside is to see the energy that goes into revenge as appropriate self-protection against sudden changes in the weather.)

As we will describe in Chapter 6, energy is frequently diverted from goal-oriented activities to survival-oriented activities, or distributed so widely that no progress can be made. This is analogous to living in a hostile climate where most of people's time and energy is spent in keeping up with where they are—in surviving—and consequently very little energy goes into progress-related activities. The most graphic weather analogy is shovelling snow during a heavy storm—just as you get a path cleared, it's time to shovel the additional accumulation. By the end of the day you have managed to wind up where you were the day before.

Another source of diverted energy is the large start-up time and/or energy required in many systems. We have had clients describe their work lives as one long series of start-up periods (getting ready to work on a new project or team) and phasing-out periods, interspersed with short, momentary flashes of production. This may be true of many systems, because of our relatively poor skills for beginning and ending relationships. What is called for is more sophistication and practice with what Bennis and Slater have termed "temporary systems": groupings that come together, organize quickly, and disperse quickly when their useful purpose has been served.[8]

Perhaps the most costly negative distribution of energy in organizations is inappropriate competition between internal units that should be collaborating if the system's goals are to be met. Speer provides a very crisp example from the German military:

Even aside from Hitler's objections, a rational course of
action such as this would have been complicated by the
fact that Peenemunde was developing the conflict of interests and the fierce ambitions of the army and the air force,
the army would never have allowed its rival to take over the
installations it had built up in Peenemunde. This rivalry
made it impossible for even research and development to
be conducted jointly (see footnotes on p. 258 in Chapter 16).
Project Waterfall could have gone into production even earlier had Peenemunde's full capacity been used in time. As
late as January 1, 1945, there were 2210 scientists and engi-
neers working on the long range rockets A-4 and A-9,
whereas only 220 had been assigned to Waterfall, and 135
to another anti-aircraft rocket project, Typhoon.[9]

The more this kind of internal in-fighting is allowed or rewarded, the more difficult it is for the larger system to use its
potential energy well.

(P) Pleasure

We call the third dimension simply "pleasure," because for
every climate (geographic or organizational) there are people
who like being in it and there are those who do not. Whether a
climate is pleasing obviously varies with the tastes and back-
ground of the person. While one person will rave about life in
Southern California, another finds it monotonous compared with
his favorite New England town, and still another declares Seattle
to have the only really good climate ("the rain keeps the dust
down...").

Organizations similarly provide climates that appeal more
to certain members than to others. The structure, the kinds of
people who are working there, the formal rules, the informal
norms, the degrees of freedom to play or experiment, the kinds
of tasks the system is doing, the physical layout of the system,
and so on all contribute to the suitability of a climate for a particular member. The reward system plays an important part in
determining the amount of pleasure an individual experiences in
an organization, particularly such informal rewards as recognition and appreciation. All of these factors affect the fit (or lack
of it) between the person and the climate. Does he or she look

"Is the ambience wrong, or do you just need to be alone?"

forward to getting there in the morning, and want to stay when given the option to go home? Does he or she stay when offered another job, or move as soon as an alternative is available? These outcomes are indicators of the amount of pleasure the person finds in the environment.

It is interesting to question the extent to which different individuals are able to change the system to make it a more pleasurable place. Some are able to "do something about the weather rather than just talk about it," while others tend to accept it as a given. We will discuss this point further in the next two chapters.

(G) Growth

The fourth and last dimension we will be using throughout the book is the extent to which the organization's climate is good for the growth of the people within the system. To continue our weather analogy, some climates are good for growing one kind of crop, some for growing another, some for not growing anything. There are tropical paradises and barren deserts, and the same is true for organizations. Douglas McGregor once likened the managerial role to tending a garden, the emphasis being on the growth and development of managers under the right conditions (climate) rather than on expecting to "make" someone develop because you want them to do so.[10]

What do we mean by growth? For one, we mean a person's development of new skills, abilities, and capacities different from those already evident. Thus, growth at any given time depends on the level a person starts at, not on any absolute scale. And "level" doesn't fully describe the concept either, since growth can be an expansion into new areas altogether, rather than getting "better" at something or rising up some ladder of success. Growth may even be the reduction in number of different activities and the focusing on a few important ones in more depth, if this is a new step for the person involved.

Organizations and groups vary markedly on how good a climate they provide for growth of their members. Many systems tend to place a great or total emphasis on rewarding performance in the short run, so that a personal cost is placed on behavioral experimentation, exploration, and other activities that lead to learning. People in this kind of climate tend to seek those activities they can already do well, in which they have facility, and to avoid newer activities where they have some chance of failing. Conversely, high-growth climates promote and encourage exploration, "stretching" activities, and provide support for people developing their potentialities. Leavitt has called this "the fertilizer approach," where one manages conditions rather than people.[11]

Of course, just as with the weather, a particular organization climate may promote growth for some people and stifle it for others. Some roles also provide more opportunities for growth-producing activities. Those whose jobs involve public contact often develop their talents more fully than persons who deal strictly with people internal to the system. A company where only the president has high-level outside contacts may be a growthful climate for the president, but a stagnating climate for other key managers.

A key diagnostic indicator of growth climates is the extent to which the climate allows for and recognizes that people have different learning styles. For example, is it openly recognized that some people respond to a high-conflict, confronting atmosphere and can use it to learn, while others are immobilized by it? Is it seen as normal that the latter type of person responds more readily to a climate of support and basic agreement, from which they move out to experiment? Many systems operate under the basic assumption that there is one pattern for growth in competence. This pattern is often operationally defined as taking the right jobs in the right sequence ("punching your tickets") and moving up in the system, in turn helping to cause the phenomenon of the Peter Principle.[12] The norms of the system dictate that anyone who wants to be a success in the organization must avoid job changes that are not "promotions" and must accept promotions when offered. Acceptance is presumed to be evidence of drive and loyalty (as well as of submissiveness to those controlling one's fate).

By contrast, an organization climate that encouraged different modes of growth would have no single definition of learning and progress and the road to success. There would be an emphasis on diagnosis, self-understanding, and exploratory actions based on what would be a next step for the *person*, not the next slot for the body at that level in the system. This would also allow for expansion of competence through moving into different job areas that might be "lateral" or "down" in terms of the organization's hierarchy. The emphasis would not be on whether it is a "higher" step, but on whether it contributes to the organization and to the growth of competence or self-understanding in the person. We believe that good choices about growth-producing situations are best made collaboratively, by the individual and members of the organization who can provide helpful information. This process is in sharp contrast to that used in many systems today, where job decisions are made from somewhere "up there," with little or no consultation with the person involved. Such consultation would destroy the decision maker's sense of being in total control of the chessboard and its players.

In essence, we are describing one factor that we feel leads to a growth-producing climate in an organization: the degree to which members are valued as contributors to decisions about the kinds of roles they play. Another factor is the reward system in the organization: Is one's survival difficult and therefore considered to be the main determinant of "success," or is there a greater emphasis on productivity? If it is productivity, is it short-run productivity (which leads people to emphasize those things they already do well) or does it include the longer-term performance of the system (which requires people to develop their latent potential) as well? This all gets communicated through such behaviors as who receives raises, who gets promoted, and who is involved in promotional decisions.

SUMMARY

The internal climate of any organization or social system has several rather distinct dimensions. Each climate has a certain amount of *energy* associated with it. The amount of energy in the system is determined largely by the norms of the system (see Chapter 4).

The *distribution of energy* within the system determines the relative amount of energy available for survival (adaptiveness), task-related production (goal attainment), maintenance (integration), and tension release (play, rituals). The question is how to find a balance; energy needs to be focused in different areas under different conditions.

The amount of energy and the distribution of energy help to determine the amount of *growth* in competence or skills of the members. The amount of growth in any given climate is partially influenced by the reward system (tolerance for failure), norms about predictability (amount of prescribed behavior which limits growth), the amount of curiosity, and the ability to take risks to learn new behavior.

Pleasure is a function of the other climate dimensions as well as the personal tastes of organization members. People who like a stressful environment are likely to thrive and grow in such a climate, whereas people who like a supportive environment are unlikely to grow in such a climate. Growth leads to pleasure, but pleasure doesn't necessarily lead to growth. High pleasure can lead to a country-club atmosphere if the energy generated by the pleasure isn't distributed into all areas, but is funneled exclusively into tension release.

In the following two chapters we will explore these four dimensions, using the metaphor of organization weather. Next, several key contributors to organization climate, including group norms, fear-inducing leadership strategies, physical settings, and patterns of information flow will be analyzed. For each concept, a descriptive chapter is followed by a chapter on changing that area of behavior. The book concludes with some ideas on how to select change strategies for various situations.

NOTES

1. Paul Lawrence and Jay Lorsch, *Developing Organizations* (Reading, Mass.: Addison-Wesley, 1969).

2. Albert Speer, *Inside the Third Reich* (New York: Macmillan, 1970), p. 91. Copyright © 1970 by Macmillan Publishing Co., Inc. Reprinted by permission.

3. Anthony Powell, *The Military Philosophers* (London: Heinemann, 1968), p. 16. Reprinted by permission.

4. P.G. Wodehouse, *Psmith in the City* (Harmondsworth, Middlesex: Penguin, 1970), p. 102. Reprinted by permission of the author's Estate and its agents, Scott Meredith Literary Agency, Inc., 845 Third Ave., New York, N.Y., 10022.

5. Robert Blake and Jane Mouton, *The Managerial Grid* (Houston: Gulf, 1964).

6. Anthony Powell, *The Soldier's Art* (London: Heinemann, 1966), pp. 60–61. Reprinted by permission.

7. Melville Dalton, *Men Who Manage* (New York: Wiley, 1959).

8. Warren Bennis and Philip Slater, *The Temporary Society* (New York: Harper & Row, 1968).

9. Albert Speer, *Inside the Third Reich*, p. 365. Copyright © 1970 by Macmillan Publishing Co., Inc. Reprinted by permission.

10. Douglas McGregor, *The Human Side of Enterprise* (New York: McGraw-Hill, 1960).

11. H.J. Leavitt, "Beyond the Analytic Manager, Part II," *California Management Review* 17, no. 4 (Summer 1975): 20.

12. Simply put, that people tend to be promoted through the system until they rise to a level where they are not competent. See Lawrence J. Peter and Raymond Hull, *The Peter Principle* (New York: Morrow, 1969).

Chapter 2

Everybody Talks about the Weather

In this chapter, by further exploring our weather metaphor, we hope to uncover new analogues for the nature of organizational life. We do not propose any magical connection between the two kinds of climate, nor do we consider the following discussion to be a "proof" of anything in particular. Our main purpose is simply to examine the notion of weather in an organizational context and see what we can learn about the causes and effects of organization climate. Hopefully, leaders and other members of organizations will find the discussion helpful in perceiving the climates in which they work and which they help to create for other people.

THE FEEL OF A PLACE

One of our first approaches to organization weather is the simple question of what it *feels* like to be in different climates: Does an organization have a characteristic "feel" as does a geographic location? Anyone who has worked in or visited a number of organizations would have to agree that they do. In certain organizations it always feels gray and overcast, as if clouds are blocking whatever potential sunshine is around. In others, the basic pattern seems to be sunshine and warmth, as far as social interaction is concerned. Some systems feel muggy and humid, and one can never quite get comfortable in them. There are many other ways of describing the "feel" of a system, probably limited only by our abilities to be aware of our own immediate

"Feels like another one of those ho-hum days."

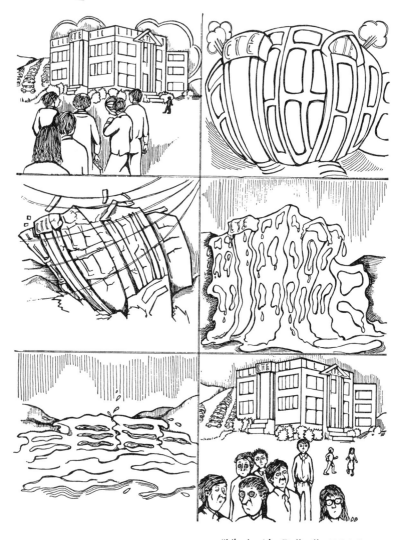

"Like I said—Dullsville, U.S.A."

experiences.[1] Some are stormy, some calm, some windy, some only intermittently gusty; some feel alive, some dead, some growing, and some stagnant.

The concept of comfort is also closely linked to organization climate and feel. Comfort is the result of both the *kind of climate* and the *preferences of the individual.* The comfortable organization climate for one person may be impossibly stuffy (or hectic) for someone else. In addition, comfort (or pleasure) is only one dimension for describing effects of a climate. A place may be comfortable for a person and at the same time stifle his or her growth or productivity; conversely, it may be both comfortable and stimulating.

Most readers have probably encountered systems where they experienced the continual threat of "storms" or "rain," and felt they had to wear foul-weather gear (or psychological overcoats) all the time to be ready for any inclemency that might occur. After a time, this "long winter" begins to weigh one down, until it seems like the weight of one's overcoat has permanently bent the back into a stoop. In many organizations and roles the psychological overcoat is felt to be required; its wearing is a continuous process that may be noticed less and less, but whose effect is actually greater and greater in terms of permanently bending the individual. To the extent that protective gear seems always necessary, the person assumes that certain stances, positions, actions, and risks are just not prudent to take. After a long period this check on behaviors becomes unconscious, and the loss of other possibilities is no longer noticed; the constraints are soon to be a permanent part of his or her "real world." A climate that requires continuous protection for survival will tend to have uneven distribution of energy into threat-reducing activities and away from growth and production-oriented ones. Constant maintenance of "just in case" files is an example.

For example, in one case where executives were managing by detail, the subordinates created the 'JIC' file, which stands for: (just in case) some superior asks. This file was kept up to date by several lower-level managers who were full time and countless other people working part time. The JIC file is an organizational defense against threat experienced by individuals at various levels.[2]

TYPES OF INCLEMENCY

It should be possible to categorize the types of bad weather a particular organization experiences. Some have storms that shoot through the system, raging as they go, such as the massive management shake-ups experienced by many organizations during cyclic recessions of the economy. Other organizations have storms with a calm at the center—while some people remain unaffected, others are battered at the storm's edges. Some have damp periods followed by clearing and drying. Others endure a continual drizzle that never seems to let up, so that many members always feel vaguely "in trouble." Some storm fronts remain stationary for months, while in other systems they move in and out more rapidly. (Although we are talking about internal organization climate, it is worth mentioning that many types of inclemency may be caused by external factors as well as internal factors.)

The effects of storms vary from system to system. In some you can feel that the storms and rain are clearing the air, providing vital water for the crops (e.g., confrontations and needed energy for resolution). In others, you can sense that storms tend to beat down and destroy the crops. Storms and conflict in a system are not inherently good or bad, just as periods of calm are not—it depends on how they are used by the people in the system.

The various kinds of inclemency have fitting organizational analogues. For example, conflicts can be thought of as rain, poor communication as fog, pessimists as clouds, degree of emotionality as wind velocity, etc. It then becomes much easier to see what storms are made of. However, the elements constituting the storms are necessary to some degree for crops to grow and to make the good weather periods more usable.

Just as there are different types of inclemency, certain regions are havens from bad organizational weather. Some parts of the organization are generally turbulent, some changeable, and some predictably calm. These last often tend to be the "Floridas" of the system—the places those people go who are ready for psychological retirement even though they may have many years before they can do so officially. When there is individual influence over career decisions (which too seldom is the case), people tend to drift toward those areas that have a degree of stimulation comfortable for them.

PREDICTABILITY

Another interesting aspect of a system's weather is the notion of seasons and the cycles that an organization's climate may go through. Old hands in a system can often tell you when the next phase of loosening or tightening, of centralization or decentralization will occur, as if these were literally seasonal changes. A season for one system may last two years, for another system it may be only two months; and people can be more or less aware of the seasons through which they pass. Having seasons, or variations in climate, may be one way in which a climate remains invigorating. This cyclical change is an aspect of New England that we love — it has both regularity, stirring good feelings associated with past times, and variety, which keeps us active. When visiting in a southern climate, we found that a long string of beautiful days made us crave some change, even if not as "good" in terms of sunny outlook.

Regular seasons add to the predictability of a system's climate, and some people seem to be better than others at predicting how the system's seasons will change. These "weather forecasters" are often used to prepare others for sudden shifts. Sometimes forecasters can be identified by the number of successful subordinates they have trained and sent out to other parts of the system. In all probability, they have trained their proteges to read cues accurately concerning changes in climate and to be ready to adapt to them.

THE FEEL OF RAIN

One phenomenon that has always interested us is the extent to which the "feel" of weather is not necessarily a good indicator of its usefulness. The best example of this is rain, which is felt by many to be "bad" weather: it is uncomfortable, it curtails outdoor activities, and it can create a sense of gloom if it goes on for a long time. Yet at the same time rain is essential to growth and life; and if it is not too heavy, it is functional to the life systems it supplies with water.

The analogy between this process and organizational life seems quite clear. If we think of conflict, differences of opinion, or issues that interrupt smooth day-to-day operations as the "rain" in a system, then our and others' observations indicate

"Relax, Perkins, we've all made inaccurate forecasts—alot of people are glad it didn't rain."

that many people find this rain uncomfortable and gloomy. Avoidance of conflict is a very common pattern in organizations of all kinds. And this is where the "feel" of discomfort is not an accurate guide to how one should function. As Blake and Mouton point out, conflict and differences are the "water" that stimulates and nourishes growth as well as creative resolution of difficult choices.[3] Conflict can stimulate learning from experience rather than continuing to operate at less than full potential. Of course, it can rain so much, with so many conflicts and differences, that positive action is blocked, there is a "flood," and the system suffers. But in most systems, the problem tends to be a lack of nourishing conflict: there may be too little "rain" type of conflict, or the conflict that exists cannot be handled well by the system and consequently is detrimental.

We should also add that, just as certain people find rain invigorating, there are also those who do not find open conflict gloomy. They are stimulated by it and their natural tendency is to use it as a trigger for dealing with necessary issues. We believe that most people can to some extent be stimulated by conflict, and this capacity can be developed through strategies such as those described in the later chapters of this book, just as people who move from the city to the country often discover they have a latent love for rain. (Their new setting allows them to enjoy its positive features.)

CHANGEABILITY

A dimension of organization weather that has been implied in several of the above discussions is changeability—the extent to which a system feels pretty much the same over time or undergoes wide swings in mood. Whether it is more or less useful for the climate to be stable remains an open question. Stability is one way of having predictability, which can be useful; on the other hand, changes in climate can be stimulating and energizing, so that variations can help one avoid the feeling of being in a rut.

Related to changes of seasons is the interesting phenomenon that occurs when the weather goes from bad to better, such as near the end of a hard winter. Spring shoots appear, sometimes a bit too early, only to be buried by the next snowstorm. This process occurs in social-change processes as well. Early changes in a system are very encouraging; expectations shoot up, only to be disappointed as regressions occur and it becomes apparent that the system cannot change so swiftly.

The point is that when major changes in climate are begun, regressions and increased dissatisfactions are predictable, and should be used as sources of energy rather than as indicators that change is unwarranted and unwanted. (This is a theme often heard in American politics these days. The dissatisfaction of minorities, the poor, or the young can be interpreted as hatred of American society *or* as disappointment generated by unmet high expectations about what the society could achieve.) These temporary regressions are a normal part of the developmental process and can be seen as developmental regressions. Children often exhibit developmental regressions and engage in more "childish" behavior just prior to moving on to a new developmental level (e.g., adolescence). The apparent regression may, in fact, be a kind of regrouping or gathering of energy for the big push to the next developmental level. It is important to view these regressions in the proper perspective. Just as a relapse of winter in the springtime is greeted with resentment and pessimism, developmental regressions in people and organizations are often unduly discouraging.

PERCEIVING ALTERNATIVE CLIMATES

It is often difficult for people who have grown up in only one kind of climate to realize that there are other possibilities in the world. For instance, some residents of California or Florida have never lived through the transitions to spring, winter, or fall, and have never seen snow falling. It is very difficult to describe these processes vividly enough to help such a person really feel what they are like.

It is similarly difficult to help people become aware of other possibilities in organizational climate. In our own research, when interviewing people in a particular company, we often hear comments such as, "You have to watch out what you say and never raise an issue with your boss in public, which causes me some problems. But that's the way it is in business, isn't it?" These people are asking us to confirm their view that there are no other kinds of climate than the one they are experiencing. This is especially noticeable when an individual has spent his or her whole working life with one company, government agency, church, or whatever. Perhaps organizations should institute a policy of regular travel or trips to other kinds of organizations with very different kinds of climates—a kind of "grand tour" periodically to stimulate perception of the range of alternatives. This does assume, however, that the organization's leaders *want* to work toward having a range of climates for people with different needs, and toward exploring new climates. If this commitment is not present and the system is not prepared to accept members being aware of other possibilities, then such outside exploration is inadvisable.

POLLUTION

Another aspect of the physical environment analogous to the social-system climate is pollution. Twentieth-century man in the age of technology has assumed that he could do what he wished to the physical environment with few repercussions. This view has recently begun to change drastically, as people now realize we are beginning to pay the delayed costs of a hundred years of dumping industrial wastes into rivers, lakes, and oceans. If we do not continue to pay increased attention to the pollution of our physical environment, we will have to contend with vastly reduced resources. Some lakes, such as Lake Erie, are already biologically dead.

A similar view is now becoming more clear in organizational theory. Writers such as Gardner[4] and researchers such as Likert[5] are warning that if an organization does not concern itself with the pollution of its internal human climate, it will probably not survive in the long run and will not be vigorous enough to meet high performance standards in the short run. We must create organizational climates that promote the growth and stimulation of human beings, rather than continue with climates that tend to produce stagnation, alienation, and withdrawal.

INFLUENCEABILITY

Be assured we do not intend to stay locked on the weather metaphor continuously—we do not consider it by any means perfectly descriptive of organization climate. It begins to break down if one thinks of it in strictly physical terms, for people tend to *talk* about physical weather but don't *do* anything, because they feel relatively powerless to affect it. Even here the metaphor is instructive, though, for many organization members treat organization climate the same way—they endow it with a physical actuality and inevitability that implies they are powerless to change it. In many instances they are right, if attempts are made with no coordination. But if people can get together and examine the climate of their system collaboratively, they have the potential for making it significantly different and more in line with their desires.

Organization Development (OD) programs usually have climate change as one of their implicit or explicit goals. Such efforts are generally directed at cultural change within the organization and employ techniques designed to alter the norms and behaviors of organization members. Successful OD programs are those in which people are operating on the assumption that they *can* change the weather by working together toward specific goals. Some climates are more resistant to change than others and the degree of resistance is partially dependent on the degree to which people see the system as open to influence. Even very large (and hence very bureaucratic) organizations can change their climate if enough members want the change and believe it can be done. The massive change in the climate and operation of the Democratic Party between 1968 and the present is a good illustration. The issues surrounding climate change will be discussed generally in the next chapter, and for specific change areas throughout the book.

SUMMARY

Organization climate can be thought of in terms of the weather. Some organizations have predictably sunny climates (low demands), while others seem always to encounter storms with lots of precipitation (conflict) and fog (poor communication). Unlike the physical weather system, the organization weather system can be influenced if its pattern is understood. Some storms are natural and merely signal the onset of a new season, while others are potentially dangerous and need to be stopped before damage is done. Good weather forecasters in the system can tell the difference and signal the kind of response called for. Without some specific attention being paid to the organization's weather system and its management, people often feel they must protect themselves from unforeseen inclemency by donning psychological foul-weather gear.

Much valuable energy can be expended protecting oneself from the weather, and such activities also cut down on a person's pleasure and growth in an organization. If an individual finds a particular weather system incompatible with his or her life style, a different climate should be sought out. In certain systems, however, nearly everyone seeks protection—these organizations have highly changeable weather with lots of storms, much flood damage, little growth, and no pleasure. These climates are discussed further in Chapter 6, "Fear as a Special Climate."

NOTES

1. A Stanford psychiatrist has recently developed a series of "social climate scales" to help people assess the "feel" of their work settings. See Rudolph H. Moos, *Evaluating Treatment Environments: A Social Ecological Approach* (New York: Wiley, 1974).

2. Chris Argyris, *Interpersonal Competence and Organizational Effectiveness* (Homewood, Illinois: Dorsey, 1962), p. 48. Reprinted by permission.

3. R. Blake and J. Mouton, "Country Club Management," in *The Managerial Grid* (Houston: Gulf, 1964).

4. John Gardner, *Self-Renewal* (New York: Harper & Row, 1963).

5. Rensis Likert, *The Human Organization* (New York: McGraw-Hill, 1967).

Chapter 3

Changing the Weather

As noted before, weather is not a totally appropriate metaphor for organization climate systems, because we believe that, unlike weather, these systems *can* be influenced. Many of us rely on others to tell us what the climate is like; we do not trust our own senses to tell us what is going on and what part we play in causing it, or can play in changing it. This chapter looks at various ways of both sensing and changing climates we work in.

SENSING YOUR CLIMATE

Many people become so accustomed to their particular climate that they are practically unaware of it. A person growing up in London is likely to assume that an umbrella is a normal part of one's clothing. Similarly, people who have spent most of their work lives in one organization tend not to be aware of the climate within their organization, nor are they aware of any alternative climates. Members of a system often become overdependent on their "weather forecasters" and cease to learn for themselves new ways of being aware of social climate. They stop observing the impact of climate on individual and group functioning and they lose sight of the causes of social climate. It becomes all too easy then to think of social-system climate as if it were determined totally from the outside. Therefore, before exploring ways of changing the weather, it is necessary to explore some ways of *sensing* the weather in one's own system.

Talking to Others

We have found the metaphor of weather to be helpful in stimulating a person's perceptions about their organization's weather system. We have tried this when consulting with a new client system. Saying something over lunch like, "Gee, this place seems to be bustling with energy and activity—like there's a lot of sunshine," or "Communication within this organization seems fuzzy and unclear—like being in a fog," will usually encourage insightful feedback. If you tie those perceptions to the weather metaphor, it stimulates the generation and articulation of further perceptions. Talking with a number of people in an organization in these terms will help you develop a feel for the climate very quickly and will serve as a check on your own observations.

Cataloging

By looking over events that have occurred in the organization in terms of the weather metaphor and cataloging them in terms of rainstorms (conflict), wind storms (too much emotionalism), hurricanes (highly emotional, serious conflicts), etc., you will help to sharpen your focus on the kinds of weather phenomena characteristic of your system. You may find that there aren't any storms—in fact, there isn't even any rain. Or you may find that although the sun is shining all the time, there isn't enough breeze to keep things from becoming oppressive. In cataloging events, be sure to cover a long enough period of time to include all the different kinds of weather that tend to occur. You might find it helpful to ask someone else to do this exercise independently, and then compare what you come up with. Of course, groups can easily engage in this activity as well. In any case, the activity itself helps to raise one's consciousness about what's going on in the organizational climate one lives in.

Identifying

Closely related to cataloging events is identifying seasons. You may find, in your catalog of events, identifiable patterns that occur regularly or predictably on a daily, weekly, monthly, quarterly, or annual basis. Perhaps these events are linked to fiscal events, like the day's receipts or month-end closing. Perhaps they are linked to external phenomena like a supplier's failure to deliver promised material. Perhaps they are identifiable but entirely unpredictable, like a tornado. The degree to which you can identify patterns, cycles, or seasons in your climate is the key to understanding the climate system in an overall sense. Once the climate has been explored in depth and has been understood, it is easier to see its causes and to invent ways to change the weather if that is what is wanted.

WHICH CLIMATE IS BEST?

Just as it is possible to classify different types of geographical climate through such dimensions as temperature ranges, mean precipitation, humidity, and prevailing winds, we can classify organization climates. There is not one "best" organization climate, just as there is no single geographical climate suitable for everyone—"best" depends on the climate/person interaction. Some people love the sunny Southwest; others can't stand it. Some people love the variability of New England; others don't like the unpredictability.

When thinking about influencing organization climate, one must consider that any change in the climate will make some people happy and others angry. Other social scientists, such as McGregor, Blake, and Likert, have identified important elements of organization climate which seem to have broad appeal: Theory Y[1]; High concern for both people and production (9, 9)[2]; and System IV[3]. Yet, some people are more comfortable in organization climates other than these. Independent entrepreneurs who want to make their own impact in a much more personalized manner than is possible in a Theory Y or System IV type of organization are an example. The same can be said for bureaucrats who are looking for a highly structured climate with few demands and high predictability and security. In learning about what causes organization climate and how to influence and change it, care must be taken not to assume that the particular kind of climate you like is one everyone will like.

In our discussion of diagnosing and changing climate, some words appear to be value laden and thereby to bias an objective search for alternatives. We must admit that we are biased toward a particular set of climate conditions favoring personal freedom, initiative, and some changeability over unyielding structure, predictability, and stability. This does not make our preferences the best climate even for a majority of people.

DIAGNOSING WHAT'S WRONG

Assuming you have analyzed your climate along the lines suggested earlier in this chapter, and have kept an open mind about what's best for your particular organizational system, the following discussion should help you diagnose what (if anything) is wrong with your climate, and whether it should be changed. The weather most often feels uncomfortable when there is a poor fit between two variables. A "clammy" organization, like a clammy climate, is a good illustration. In physical weather, the poor fit is between temperature and moisture content in the air; in organizations it may be between variables such as time pressure (temperature) to achieve results, and unresolved conflict (humidity), which is blocking achievement of desired results. The higher the time pressure, the hotter the climate: the longer the conflict blocking progress exists, the more humid the climate. Hot, humid climates feel muggy and clammy.

Although any two weather dimensions can be looked at together (temperature and humidity, wind velocity and level of precipitation, temperature and wind velocity, etc.), in fact the feel of a place is a result of the interaction of all dimensions. For purposes of diagnosing what's wrong with a given climate, it is helpful to simplify things by looking only at two dimensions at any one time. The metaphor employed is that of looking at the weather through several different "windows." Only a few will be discussed here, but readers who find the approach interesting and useful are urged to make their own windows by placing any two variables on opposite sides of a simple matrix.

The Constraints Window

One of the best ways of diagnosing what's wrong in a climate is to look closely at the constraints that exist in the system in terms of both number and kind. What keeps you from doing what you'd like to do? What is preventing you from chang-ing things? Often the constraints people feel in a system are more imagined than real. The interaction of the constraints that do exist with various other dimensions, such as time pressure, can generate a particular type of weather. The following boxes describe the feel of four such climates:

Constraints

		Few	Many
Pressure for Results	High	Challenging; invigorating	Muggy; stifling
	Low	Calm; retirement village	Predictable; stable

The Pressure Window

Another complaint we frequently hear relates to pres-sure—usually time pressure. Looking at the weather through the pressure window may help to clarify the source of the pressure. (We often find that the pressure people feel is self-generated.)

Time Pressure

		Reasonable demands	Excessive demands
Pressure for Results	High	Challenging, invigorating	Stormy, much rain and wind
	Low	Sunny, calm	Humid, stifling

The Predictability Window

Sometimes weather systems are so changeable that their unpredictability feels chaotic. This window illustrates how varying degrees of predictability in the weather are likely to affect people. To illustrate, in a climate where there is high pressure to "produce," but inconsistent and changing rules for determining what is, in fact, a high level of production, fear is frequently the dominant feeling. While maintaining pressure to produce, the definition of production may shift unpredictably from "sell all you can" to "sell at the highest price you can" to "sell only what we have in inventory." In a more predictable system, the different definitions may apply predictably at different times of the year (seasons).

Predictability

		High	Low
Pressure for Results	High	Causes challenge	Causes fear
	Low	Causes calm	Causes frustration

The Change Window

This window is a modification of one invented by Ruma[4] to assess targets for change in organizations. Once you have determined which parts of your climate have healthy impact and which parts do not, it would seem logical to push for changing the unhealthy parts. The change window is an essential additional diagnostic step before actually implementing change, because in every organization there are certain areas where real constraints in the system make change impossible.

Change

	Climate that is healthy	Climate that is unhealthy
Possible to change the weather	Natural growth areas	Targets for change
Not possible to change the weather	A nice (but rare) occurrence	Fear-based climates (see Chapter 6)

Some Final Thoughts

Diagnosis is at least half the solution to changing the weather. As a final step in the diagnostic process, we would like to return to the four dimensions of climate explored in the first chapter. They can provide a useful checklist for analyzing the climate in your own system.

1. *What is the total energy level* of the system? How vital or passive is it and its members?

2. *How is energy distributed* in the system? Does the climate encourage actions aimed predominantly at protection/survival, production/growth, or some mixture of these?

3. *How much pleasure* do people get from being in this climate? Do they stay or leave; are they present when they do not have to be?

4. *How good a place is this climate for growth of people and groups?* Which kinds of people tend to grow in competence here and which kinds tend to stagnate or regress? Does this growth pattern also have implications for the long-term health of the organization, as well as the mental health of its individual members?

DOING SOMETHING ABOUT THE WEATHER

As discussed in the following chapter, norms and the organization's norm structure are very important components and determinants of climate. Therefore, learning about changing norms (Chapter 5) is the most productive approach we have found to doing something about the weather. Nevertheless, we would like to provide an overview to the question of improving organization climate by again using our weather metaphor. Obviously, the way to do something about the weather is to change one of its component variables—temperature, precipitation, wind velocity, etc.

Stirring Up a Breeze

Sometimes just talking openly about what is wrong (and right) in the climate has the effect of increasing the level of emotionality in the system. If you have ever criticized the Southern California weather to a Southern Californian, you probably have stirred up a breeze! Other methods of raising the level of emotionality in climates suffering from a lack of sufficient breeze involve taking risks by being more straightforward about your own emotions. The norms against "rocking the boat" in many systems prevent people from showing much in the way of feelings. Thus, anyone who actually shows anger when angry, joy when happy, etc. is seen as misbehaving or perhaps as stirring up a breeze.

Seeding the Clouds

Cloud seeding causes rain (conflict) which both clears the air and provides water for growth. This is a little like provoking conflict, but often it is a means of starting a natural process. Conflict does not exist (at least openly) in a system unless it is legitimized. Therefore, seeding the clouds involves making it legitimate for people to talk openly about areas of disagreement. One place to start is to make it legitimate for people to discuss candidly those elements in the climate that give them problems. In the initial phase, it may seem that you are creating a storm with only negative effects, but if the information is listened to

"I know all about the winds of change—I just don't think he's the right elf for the job."

and serious attempts are made to deal with the issues raised, the results will be beneficial. (See Chapter 11 on improving the flow of information.)

Seeking Allies

The processes of stirring up a breeze or seeding the clouds can become very lonely and frustrating if you are trying to initiate them by yourself. Weather systems are so large that at best you can only affect one small part at a time. Seeking allies has two benefits: it distributes the energy for change over a larger base, and the activities themselves can become a source of pleasure and growth for those involved. If you have ever been involved in redecorating your living space, you know the kind of excitement for change that can be generated by having others join in the process. Sometimes potential allies become real allies once you have taken the initial risks involved in stirring up a breeze or seeding the clouds. If your initial efforts have met with success, or at least have not been rejected, interested bystanders may be converted to active participants.[5]

Speed of Change

Another aspect of climate change is that different people and groups are able to stand different rates of change. In this connection, one can think of the "bends," a very painful affliction that occurs when a deep-sea diver returns too quickly to the surface. In essence, his environment has changed more quickly than the internal processes of his body can adapt. If he comes up more slowly, his body adjusts in stages. Human beings can function at widely different pressures *if* their systems have the opportunity to adjust gradually to them.

The same is true of organizations. Some people and groups need more time to adjust than others, and when the total organization climate is changing, some conscious attention must be paid to the change process for subunits and individuals so that they do not suffer from the bends. Also, since an organization is an interconnected system, the bends can occur in either direction—when the surrounding system changes faster than a subgroup or when a subgroup's climate changes faster than the surrounding system's and leads to attempts by the larger system to damp out the change.

Moving On

No discussion of climate change would be complete without looking at the alternative most often used in dealing with a bad fit between a person and a geographic climate: the person moves to a more acceptable region. We believe people can influence an organization climate and change it to be more generally invigorating. Nevertheless, there will always be individuals who cannot adjust to a particular organization's climate. In those instances, we think a person should seriously consider moving to another "region" (system) that fits him or her better.

In all too many cases, it is considered a failure on either the person's or the organization's part if such a change occurs, and "turnover" is whispered in threatening tones. In our view, it should be just the opposite. It should be legitimate for someone to move on, and he or she should not have to hide the fact that a move is being considered. Too often any move is explained away as simply "more money" or " he wasn't any good anyway," while the system's climate factor is carefully ignored or even denied directly. Only through legitimizing moves and discussing them openly can an organization learn from the instances of mismatch between its climate and individual styles.

NOTES

1. Douglas McGregor, *The Human Side of Enterprise* (New York: McGraw-Hill, 1960).

2. R. Blake and J. Mouton, *The Managerial Grid* (Houston: Gulf, 1964).

3. R. Likert, *The Human Organization* (New York: McGraw-Hill, 1967).

4. This is a slight modification of Steven Ruma's Amenability to Change Window, which he has presented at numerous conferences.

5. For some suggestions on how to develop allies, see Sam Culbert's *The Organizational Trap (And How to Get Out of It)* (New York: Basic Books, 1974).

Chapter 4

Social Norms and Organizational Climate

A very potent force in creating a climate for people working in different kinds of organizations is the system's set of social norms. By norms we mean unwritten rules that are felt to govern what people should or should not do (in behavior) or be (in attitudes) in order to be acceptable members in good standing of a particular social system. A norm is an expectation of what a "good" member of a group will be like on certain dimensions. The norms of an organization or other social system (family, club, school) have a major effect on the kind of weather that exists in that system. That is, norms help determine the amount of *energy* in that system, the *distribution* of energy, and the amount of *pleasure* and *growth* in that system.

The primary function norms play is to lend some stability and predictability to the behavior of group members. Norms limit the range of possible things that can happen at any given instant, and so help provide identity and thrust to the group's actions. Every social system with any connection between members must have some norms to differentiate members from non-members.

Although the existence of norms is neither good nor bad *per se*, in practice different groups have different normative patterns. These tend to have different impacts on the climate and effectiveness of the group—some better and some worse. This chapter examines the nature of norms and their relationship to climate.

SOME ATTRIBUTES OF NORM SYSTEMS

Groups vary widely in the kinds of norms they have and in the number of different areas of behavior or attitudes covered by specific norms. In other words, not all behaviors have norms or guidelines associated with them in a particular group. One group may have fairly strong norms about smoking or not smoking, as the case may be, whereas another group will have no rules about smoking and behavior in that area is left up to the individual. The same is true in other areas, such as what should or should not be worn to work, the acceptability of beards, etc. Often these norms are very strong, even though no one knows who started them or why they exist in the system (i.e., what purpose they serve).

In one client company we observed elaborate dress norms that were noticeable only to a visitor or new member, just as the weather in a particular region is more noticeable to an outsider. These included norms about when it was acceptable to wear white shirts or colored shirts to work; what parts of the organization allowed sport coats and slacks; acceptable materials for suits; when it was all right to come to work without a tie (during the annual plant shutdown period, managers could come to work without a tie and during that time *no one* wore a tie); and so on.

One test of whether a norm exists or not is to look at what happens when someone varies from a pattern of behavior that has been regular for the group. This is necessary because there are both behavior *patterns* and *norms* in groups, which both look like norms until they are violated. When a simple pattern of behavior is broken, nothing much happens to the group or the person that violates it. On the other hand, when a norm is violated, others tend to feel resentful or uneasy and they respond with some behavior designed to let the person know he or she has deviated from the norm. This may take the form of an open sanction or punishment, such as telling the person he or she is out of bounds, ignoring the individual, or other kinds of moves well known to all of us. More subtle enforcement, such as joking, kidding, or warning the person lightly about other norm violators, may also be used. In sum, norms are standards for behavior that must be adhered to if one wishes to keep in good standing in the group, and can vary widely depending on the nature of the group or the organization.

For illustrative purposes, Table 4.1 shows some of the self-described norms that a group from one large company listed after spending a week in a management seminar. They contain both *prescriptions* ("dos") and *proscriptions* ("don'ts"). They deal with both *behaviors* and with *attitudes,* although operationally they almost all are enforced or measured through behaviors. Short of mind reading, groups have to use behavior as their basic data for making inferences about attitudes (e.g., "*look* like you're getting something out of it").

Table 4.1
Norms of a Seminar Group (listed by the group)

Wear coats to meals.

Keep your same seat (early).

Change your seat (today).

Be "polite" to the outside speaker (in for the day).

Be frank with others.

One person speak at a time.

No one talk too much of the time.

No one talk about certain areas: inside people, motives, age, the formal leader, one's self.

Put in a full work day at regular work hours.

Look like you're getting something out of it (the seminar).

Don't "divert" the topic of conversation.

Stay together outside the formal sessions — eat together, at the bar, etc.

Look awake.

Test the outside speaker.

Keep profanity low (or at the speaker's level).

Modulate criticisms so that they don't sound harsh.

Listen to one another.

Put your comments in the right "form" (which is how others want to hear them).

Flagellate the company and its mistakes.

But sound loyal underneath it all.

Wear shoes in the meetings.

Be nonemotional.

Don't look "foolish"; look competent.

In terms of the goals they had as a group (learning about organization and management, and expanding their own self-understanding), they saw some of these norms as creating a *facilitative* climate for reaching their goals (e.g., "Listen to one another"; "Be frank with others") and other norms as creating an *inhibitive* climate that blocked them (e.g., "Don't talk about certain areas..."; "Don't look foolish, look competent."). Finally, they saw that some of their norms were *conscious* ones that had more or less been chosen openly by the group ("Wear coats to work"; "One person speak at a time") with some discussion, and that other norms were *unconscious* ones that evolved over time without any discussion of their benefits and costs to the group ("Be polite to the outside speaker"; "Modulate criticisms so that they don't sound harsh"). For this group, as for many others, the bulk of their norms were unconscious ones that had evolved over time without any reexamination.

While discussing these in an open meeting, it also became clear that there were varying degrees of *commitment* and *agreement* to the various norms they identified. Some norms were agreed on, but with little commitment—there was a low intensity of feeling about maintaining them. For others, there was not even agreement about what the norm should be, and only part of the group thought it important. Still other norms that were listed turned out to be *patterns*, as described earlier—that is, they were uniform ways of doing things in the group that turned out to be apparent rather than real rules. There was no feeling of resentment or attempt to apply sanctions when someone deviated from them (e.g., "Wear shoes in the meetings.").

SOURCES OF NORMS

We said earlier that norms serve the function of providing predictability for group actions. But how do they come into existence in the first place? One source of norms is the *culture of the country* in which the organization exists. Cultural norms arise from the language, tradition, and heritage of the country. We all have mental images of the "typical" Frenchman, Italian, Mexican, and how he or she behaves (i.e., what some of his or her rules for behavior are). Geographic regions within countries also are a source of norms. The standard types of behavior vary somewhat from, say, Southern California to the South's "Bible Belt," and people travelling from one region to another experience differences in degrees of formality, kinds of appropriate greetings, and so on.

A second source of norms for any particular organization's internal climate is the *overall work culture* of the society. What are the society's norms about how people behave in the world of work? For instance, many norms are considered to be general ways of doing things in business, and these often can become very potent sources of control over people's behavior.

A third source of norms for an individual is the *organization to which she or he belongs*. Each organization has to some degree its own unique culture or set of norms. People who change jobs and move to a different organization are often able to describe very clearly some of the fundamental differences in basic climate or norms between the two organizations. One organization may be very careful about problems of ethics, reciprocity, and similar areas, whereas another may have norms that stress output and encourage its members to make deals however they can. Organizational norms are partly dependent on the organization's mission. The norm system for a business-products company usually covers different areas than one in a research organization, government agency, or community-action organization.

Finally, within the organization's normative system, certain norms are developed by *particular groups*. These norms usually relate to more specific matters: what kinds of things can and cannot be talked about in that particular group; who spends time with whom at lunch or other informal break times; and how different spaces should be allocated and used by people, such as where meetings can and cannot be held. Most of these latter norms are determined by a person's primary work group, but these group norms are also influenced by the kinds of previously held assumptions members bring to the group, including their notions about what "work" is generally supposed to be (e.g., the Protestant Ethic, or a fair day's work for a fair day's pay), and norms that exist in the broader organization—such as those governing dress, work on weekends, etc.

One interesting aspect of these different sources of norms is that people who form a new group in an organization on a temporary basis often carry into that group such a large set of shared assumptions about the way they should behave that their group behavior is governed by "invisible" norms. As a result, new alternatives are rarely considered. The more often people assume that something is a "natural law"—such as the "law" that people should stay seated when they are in a group meeting—the more their assumptions tend to become invisible, and therefore not conscious to the members nor very open to their control.

Just as the weather is governed by "unchangeable" natural law, invisible assumptions make organizational climate *seem* unchangeable. Group members may talk about the climate and what it feels like to be there, but if they are unable to trace the climate back to particular assumptions, norms, or rules of the game, they cannot influence it. Inability to influence climate often leads to a sense of futility, frustration, and anger at the lack of control over one's own fate. The climate becomes another given of the situation.

Norms develop both consciously (such as through a discussion of why it's important to be on time for work in the mornings) and unconsciously (as when a group tends to wait for one elder member to start the discussion, as a kind of invocation). The majority of norms in most groups evolves unconsciously from a group standpoint. That is, individual members may be aware of them, but there is little or no open discussion of the norms' consequences, such as whether they facilitate or block individual or group performance.

Many norms are in fact historical accidents, which each person assumes others feel strongly about. Someone may have had a bad experience at some point and everyone assumes a norm exists against whatever that person did. This is not discussed openly, nor are the underlying assumptions about everyone having the same work style, so that the effects of this norm are not tested through joint exploration. A norm can become quite solidified without any real shared choice having been made. We will return to this evolutionary process in a discussion of "successive distortions" later in this chapter.

THE NATURE OF NORMS

There are numerous dimensions for describing the norms that exist in a particular group. For this discussion we will assume that although norms have different sources (as we have just indicated), we can still isolate a certain set of norms as a stable influence operating in a particular group at a particular time.

One dimension for looking at norms is the *range of acceptable behavior*. Some norms are very specific as to the kind of behavior that is acceptable, so that any acts which deviate very much from this are considered unacceptable. For other norms, the range of acceptable behavior may be quite broad, so that only extreme deviation is frowned on.

Norms also differ in terms of *intensity*. There are some normative areas or rules about which group members will feel quite strongly. Reactions tend to be drastic when such norms are violated, as with norms against nudity in many American social groupings. When this norm is violated in a business setting, the intensity of reaction and, therefore, of hostile behavior toward the deviant is quite strong. On the other hand, general norms about such things as how much people should talk in a meeting produce only mild resentment when violated, perhaps not even enough to result in anyone letting the person know he or she has broken the norm.

A third dimension of norms is their *target*. To whom in the group or organization does a particular norm apply? Some norms apply to everyone ("we should all have clothes on when we come to work"), and some apply only to particular people or roles ("the managers in the plant should wear white shirts and ties"; "the boss should not help with cleaning up"). Often the variations in norms are related to status — that is, the higher-status people in a system are judged by standards different from those applied to lower-status members.

Note that we said "different" standards. It is not as simple as saying that one or the other has more stringent norms applied to them. William Whyte found in his early study of street gangs that the leader of a gang was freer to break the minor norms of the group and behave as he pleased, yet he was also expected to be the most consistent observer of the central or major norms of the group — those considered to be the essence of its identity (e.g., that you never back down or retreat when a challenge of a fight is offered). On these major or core norms, lower-status gang members were freer to deviate than the leader, since less was expected of them.[1] Bosses in work organizations often report the same pressure, although they may describe it in their own words as "setting an example" or "exercising my authority." They feel that if they don't follow their own norms, no one else will either.

Norms apply differently to those who are full-fledged members of a system than to those who are "provisional" members. It often happens that norms are applied more strictly to new group members until they prove that they have the right motivation and will play ball with the group. Up to that point, any deviation is met with attempts to set him straight or teach him the ropes, usually with avowals that it is for *his* own good. Of course, these attempts to "help" the person are also aimed at keeping the group's system going.

ENFORCEMENT OF NORMS

The above reactions are examples of sanctions applied whenever a norm is broken. If there were no sanctions, norms could not be maintained because there would be no consequence for breaking a norm. Sanctions can be explicit or implicit and can vary in intensity.

What, in fact, does happen when people deviate from the norms of their group or organization? If no one sees it, nothing may happen (although the person may feel some personal guilt if he or she shares the norm). If it is observed, then usually some sort of reaction occurs which is aimed at signaling to the person that he or she is out of bounds, pressuring the person to get back in bounds, or sometimes supporting the violation of the norm (if the observer agrees the norm should be broken).

Sociologists have explored many facets of normative behavior and enforcement—far too many to discuss here.[2] The important point for our purposes is simply the fact that in a given group each person is an enforcer of norms for the other members. It is not enough just to understand the norms of your group in terms of how the norms feel to you; you should also become aware of the ways in which you, yourself, enforce the group's norms on other people. A kidding remark can be just as potent a control on someone's behavior as a direct "command" to stop or start doing something.

Enforcement of a norm rarely requires a total group's action. One or two people can say directly or indirectly that a person has raised a taboo issue (like salaries); and if the rest of the group is silent or changes the subject, it will feel to the target person as if the whole group had acted, even if no one else really minded. We contribute to the strength of a norm by what we are willing to let others enforce unchallenged, since our silence signals tacit approval. By both our actions and nonactions we are all enforcers and creators of the norms (and climate) that each of us feels in a group or organization.

This is particularly true for the person in a position of authority or power in a group. The boss of a work group can have a major influence on the norms of the group if he or she is considered a member (i.e., is trusted). If the boss is seen more as an adversary, then he or she probably will be able to influence only the formal rules of the system and will have little influence on the feelings (normative expectations) people have about how things should be done.

One way that total groups and organizations enforce and strengthen some of their norms is through *ritual and ceremony.* For example, ground-breaking ceremonies are frequently used as opportunities for the organization's leaders to restate their philosophy in normative terms: "We take pride in being in the forefront of technology, and the building that will rise here will provide our people with the finest facilities in the industry." The norms that are being enforced or underlined are, "Be innovative," "Technology is good," and "We take care of our people." Similarly, rituals such as quarterly employee meetings tend to enforce norms of information sharing and openness. Annual Christmas parties sometimes help to highlight such norms as, "We treat our people well," or "We're one big happy family." Rituals can also be used as sanctions when norms are broken, or as preventive measures to insure that norms are enforced. A typical example is the surprise military inspection tour of an installation. Such inspections are largely ritualistic, but are done because officers think they serve to keep people on their toes. (And to reinforce the norm of one-way control: the enlisted men never make surprise inspections of headquarters.)

EFFECTS OF NORMS

One important effect of norms is their impact on the climate of a particular work setting. Which norms are needed to create which kinds of climate? This is a necessary question to ask because people in most societal systems are unaware of or blind to most of their norms. Stop reading for a moment and select a group in which you spend considerable time (work, family, etc.).

Can you think of five norms that you consciously have thought about and evaluated before this? Try it. By spending some time at it, or by talking to others, you probably can come up with a fair list of informal rules of the game; but we doubt if you will have considered many of these norms before now.

Energy

If it is not good or bad *per se* to have norms, what kinds of general statements can be made about the impact of norms on group climate? One is that norms can affect the amount of energy stimulated by the climate. Norms about work (how hard to work, how much work is "enough," how reasonable are the demands for work) have a big effect on the amount of available energy.

For example, many organizations have seasonal demands on energy because of the nature of their work (service or product). Whether there is enough human energy available in the system to meet the seasonal demands largely depends on the norms about work. In organizations where there are strong norms about helping one another out when work piles up and about really turning out the work in periods of peak demand, energy is produced by the norms themselves and a kind of synergy exists. In terms of the weather analogy, optimal amounts of wind, rain, and sunshine give energy to the area for growth and productivity. Conversely, in organizations where hard workers are sanctioned as "rate-busters," or people who help others are considered to be encroachers, the amount of energy available for a given number of employees is severely limited.[3] The limits can be particularly restrictive if the work loads are *variable* but the norms are *rigid*: that is, there are relatively fixed rules about how much a person should produce in a day, and the rules take no account of the seasonal changes in demand.

Distribution of Energy

A second generalization is that norms affect the distribution of energy within a group or organization. Norms that place a value on teamwork tend to broaden the distribution of energy, while norms that emphasize careful individual competition and comparisons tend to encourage a distribution of energy toward

"Alright, men, get in there and create! Peters, a word in my office first."

"winning" individual contests rather than toward system performance.

Crises in one location (person or group in an organization) tend to focus energy in that location and skew its distribution, whereas norms that encourage reciprocity between people and groups help to increase the potential overall distribution of energy. People are freer to do what needs to be done without calculating in advance whether they will win or lose by the single event.

Norms with a narrow range of acceptable behavior will be experienced as more confining because they tend to focus energy on survival (fitting the norms) rather than distributing it into more spontaneous behavior. Whether this impact is desirable or not varies somewhat with different personal styles; some people will prefer this focusing of energy because it provides a clearer signal as to which behaviors are correct and "good."

Pleasure

Norms also have a large impact on the pleasure a climate provides to group members, an area perhaps more affected by norms than any other. Some of the more important norms affecting pleasure are those concerning expressiveness and those concerning play. In the area of expressiveness, norms about such behavioral characteristics as spontaneity are important (i.e., How do people react to someone who cries? Is it acceptable to act spontaneously when you feel joyful, happy, angry?). Also important are norms affecting seriousness or formality (i.e., the kinds of behavior considered "proper" in a place of business, university, church, etc.). Norms that determine when and where play is allowed also affect pleasure. For example, when a certain amount of play (e.g., joviality or humorous remarks) is allowed or even encouraged in meetings as well as during breaks and over meals, there is likely to be more pleasure in the climate. People are able to express themselves more fully as the need arises, rather than having to let off steam later.

Growth

Finally, norms often affect the amount of growth in a setting. Norms that support experimentation and risk taking (e.g., Can you talk with others when you are still tentative about something, to test it out? Or is there a norm that says you must always be "right" if you value your career?) can have a large effect on growth. The same can be said for any norms which encourage the stretching or expansion of the person's resources (job rotation, further education, sabbatical leave to try something new, etc.). Norms against trying out unformed ideas are much more costly when the group's task requires a high degree of creativity and mutual stimulation. Norms against making a mistake can be more constraining in an organization that operates in an unstable environment and therefore needs risk-taking in order to act at all.

Not all rules stifle growth. Some norms (e.g., against physical violence) provide a narrow range of acceptable behavior which creates security and lends stability to the group. This, in turn, allows the relationships to grow in new directions. Norms that encourage risk taking and discourage too-quick evaluation of personal experiments can be very helpful in promoting a growth-producing climate for individuals. In essence, the norms control the group's controls on personal experimentation.

Typical Climate Problems Caused by Norms

In some organizations, norms generally help members to be productive and enjoy their setting. Other systems tend to have norms that either cause or maintain recurring climate problems. The variety of these problems is much too great to describe completely, but we would like to share some examples of problems which may be similar to those in your own work setting.

Monotony.   When a set of norms covers many areas of behavior and has extremely narrow ranges of acceptance, everyone's behavior (including your own) tends to be predictable most of the time. Predictability has its place, but total invariability leads to a flat, dull experience in the long run, like a temperature inversion that hangs over a region for weeks and produces the same weather day after day.

Unpredictability.   This is the reverse of the monotony problem: behavior is controlled so little by the norms that there are very few patterns on which people can rely. Sometimes this is caused by lack of certain relevant norms, such as when problem-solving meetings cannot be effective because no norm says that crucial people should attend them. Another cause is the lack of effective enforcement procedures — i.e., deviance has no costs to the deviants. In this setting, the distribution of energy tends to be either self-protecting (a good strategy in the face of very little certainty about anyone else's behavior) or dissipated in actions and efforts that cancel each other out due to lack of coordination.

Untouchable Sanctity.   Some norms acquire such an aura of importance to the system that they become sacred and therefore uninfluenceable. Whether they are really crucial to life in the system can never be tested, because it is taboo to even question them. Consider the following example:

> In 1971, a writer in the British journal, *The New Statesman*, posed some questions about the Queen's "pay raise request" in light of the fact that her private income was not included in the calculations, nor is it subject to the same tax laws as other citizens. He likened it to "wanting it both ways."
>
> The newspapers responded with headlines about the fact that he had questioned the request at all: "Astonishing Attack on the Queen," etc. He had clearly violated a sacred norm against openly examining the fairness of the costs of the Monarchy, and several Members of Parliament called for an investigation of the journal — not of the issues raised in the article.

An organization cannot afford very many sacred norms if its members are going to be able to influence their own fates. As conditions change, the sacred assumption can be the Achilles' heel that drags down members' best efforts to help the system survive.[4]

Oppressiveness/Smothering.   This is the climate created by a pattern of norms which has (a) a mainly negative emphasis on what one should *not* do; (b) narrow limits as to acceptable behavior on particular norms; and (c) stiff penalties for deviance, such as loss of career advancement opportunities, loss of job, or even physical reprisals (as in Solzhenitsyn's descriptions of organizational norms for bureaucrats in *The First Circle*). The feel of this climate resembles a humid, tropical jungle, and those who have other options will tend to leave if they cannot change it, thus leaving a high proportion of people who feel not only smothered but trapped in the system.[5]

Circular or Self-Sustaining Norms. Many norms in organizations are based on some functional purpose—that is, their observance helps things to go better than they would if people did not observe them. Other norms are self-sustaining—that is, their importance is circular, depending only on their existence. (It is good to observe them because they exist and it is a good thing to observe norms.)

For example, in a food-processing plant a norm (or formal policy) about personal hair length is usually a contributor to hygenic production (and is controlled to some degree by FDA regulations). In an engineering office, a short-hair norm may be felt even more strongly, but it is its own power source; i.e., it is part of the definition of what a person should be like in order to be an "insider."

If a system has too many self-sustaining norms, there is a high probability that some of these will conflict with functional needs of the system's tasks. A classic historic example of this conflict is the United States FBI's application of strict (and very visible) dress norms to agents who, because they are trying to gain street information, wish to be inconspicuous and blend with their surroundings. It is very difficult to put street people at their ease when it is 95° in south-side Chicago and you are dressed in a grey double-knit suit, narrow dark tie, and a porkpie hat.

THE ROOTS OF NORMATIVE PROBLEMS

There are, of course, many causes for the problem patterns we have just named. We cannot describe all the causes, but we would like to focus on three related concepts we believe are crucial. These concepts help to answer the question of why a group's present normative system is not necessarily optimal from the standpoint of the climate created and its impact on effectiveness. They are: (1) successive distortions, (2) the single-reason fallacy, and (3) the lack of self-correcting processes.

Successive Distortions

Some of the norms that inhibit a group more than they help it are the result of an historical development process we call the *effect of successive distortions*. It is usually unconscious; and as a norm goes through successive distortions, it evolves through several different forms or levels.

Level A: The Functional Definition. A norm often is "born" in order to fulfill some functional need the system must meet in order to survive. For example, a small, relatively new firm in an economic crunch can't afford to hire extra resources, so a norm develops: "A good member should be committed to the system and willing to contribute extraordinary efforts in tough times, so that we can survive."

This norm has a functional purpose and can be quite helpful if people observe it. It is, however, fairly vague and not easily measured. Only individuals can know how committed they really feel inside, and "extraordinary efforts" can be defined in many ways in practice. The need for an enforceable standard creates pressure for a second-level norm to evolve.

Level B: The Operational Definition. At Level B, a normative statement provides some practical operational definition of the behavior required in Level A. To stay with our example, the Level B definition might be, "Put a lot of your waking hours into working at the company offices." This is more concrete and observable than the Level A definition, but a potential price accompanies this observability: it may encourage people *not* to do crucial tasks that would keep them away from the office and therefore risk sanctions from those who did not know they were legitimately occupied. For some norms, the distortion does not stop there. They evolve to still another level.

Level C: The Symbolic Definition. Here, the definition of valued behavior is even more measurable and therefore more enforceable. In our example, it would be something like, "Put in more than fifty hours a week at the office." This is relatively easy to observe, so that people can police one another in a general sort of way. But it goes even further toward defining "contribution" in purely quantitative, physical-presence terms that do not guarantee the company will have people doing the things that need to be done. Finally, some norms evolve another step.

Level D: The Magical Definition. This is the most operational definition, usually quantitative so that compliance can be measured on an unambiguous "yes or no" scale. Our magical definition would be, "Come into the office before 7:00 A.M. and leave after 7:00 P.M."

The four levels of evolution are summarized in the table below.

Table 4.2
Successive Distortions of Norms

Level	Definition	Example
A	Functional	"Be committed and put in extraordinary efforts."
B	Operational	"Put in long hours at the office."
C	Symbolic	"Put in more than fifty hours a week at the office."
D	Magical	"Arrive before 7:00 A.M.; leave after 7:00 P.M."

The evolution is toward more and more easily measured standards for compliance. The price for this increasing certainty about enforcement is the potential for *increasing distance of the norm from the original functional need*. The definitions become the ends in themselves, which is why we call them "symbolic" and "magical."

In the worst cases, the distorted norm can work against the original purpose, rather than just be irrelevant to it. A familiar example is the company researcher who gets a needling from office associates about not coming in until 9:30 A.M., even though he has just spent half the night at his bench completing a crucial experiment that could not be interrupted in the middle. Enforce-ment of the magical norm on him tends to encourage him not to put in necessary or extra efforts that don't fit the standard mold.

A harder-to-observe cost relates to the use of the standard of sheer physical presence as a contribution, independent of the productivity of people's activities in the 7:00 A.M. to 7:00 P.M. groove. A cadre of people reading the *Wall Street Journal* or *Village Voice* doesn't necessarily aid the system's survival, yet they fit the norm as long as they do it at the office instead of in the park.

The Single-Reason Fallacy

The evolution of successive norm distortions is supported by a shared, unconscious assumption that exists in many work groups. This can be called the single-reason fallacy and it takes this form: "If he does X, it must only mean Y." For example, if he shuts his door, it must mean he is hiding something from the rest of us. Or, if she does not come to the office until 11:00 A.M., it must be because she doesn't want to contribute to our efforts. Since groups often hold that it is bad to be secretive or noncon-tributory, norms develop to control "open door" images and arrival times.

Of course, we all know as individuals that we can close our doors for a variety of reasons: noise, wind, light, secretiveness, furniture arrangement, need for a change, etc. But collectively we enforce norms as if each act had only one possible meaning and consequence. This pattern is one of the primary sources of a rigid, oppressive organizational climate: people who behave spontaneously are punished based on others' "knowing" that they did it for only one (negative) reason—to avoid work, to hide something, or whatever. When the single-reason fallacy is in full swing, norms do more than provide predictability; they also handicap the members and force them into a "fail-safe" mode of doing only those things that can't possibly be misconstrued by anyone.

The most striking example we have found of the single-reason fallacy and its madness is described by Alexander Sol-zhenitsyn in *The Gulag Archipelago*.[6] At village meetings all townspeople, under the watchful eye of the secret police, were required to applaud as a tribute to Stalin at the beginning of the meeting. A norm quickly developed that you should not be the first person to stop applauding, since this could only occur because of your lack of zeal for the magnificent leader. The applause would go on and on, with no way of stopping, until someone stopped out of exhaustion or exasperation. A few instances of that person missing from the next meeting were enough to solidify the norm in concrete.

This norm hinged precisely on the single-reason fallacy. "The only reason someone would be the first to stop clapping is because they are disloyal to Stalin." It would not be fatigue, nor the desire to begin dealing with those matters that would help the village fulfill Stalin's plans, nor any other reason. While this is, of course, an extreme example, many similar fallacies exist in the average work group, most just as fallacious but not recognized as such.

The Lack of Self-Correcting Processes

Successive distortions and single-reason fallacies are supported by a third factor: the general lack of self-correcting processes in many groups and organizations. Many group members lack the skills to diagnose and correct recurring problems in the group's norms or other aspects of organizational process. Emotionally, they feel it is embarrassing to talk about how things don't feel right. Intellectually, they have been taught both at school and at work that it is good to focus on certain kinds of events (those having to do with the "real" work, such as how letters get filed) and bad to waste time talking about other processes ("nonwork" items, like the oppressive nature of our work climate and how we are enforcing it on one another). Chris Argyris has explored this dichotomy as part of what he calls "self-sealing systems," a characteristic of organizations whose very internal processes make it difficult for them to ever acknowledge or improve those processes.[7]

The next chapter is concerned with the issue of how to get the self-correcting process off dead center, such as challenging the self-sealing assumption that you should not talk openly about norms. We hope it will help readers to develop a greater capacity for self-correction in their own work settings.

SUMMARY

Norms are the unwritten "rules of the game": group mechanisms for social control in the human systems. They can be conscious or unconscious, facilitative or inhibitive. They can be broad or narrow in scope, and can vary widely in terms of their intensity. Organization or group norms develop as a reflection of the broader societal culture, and as a reflection of various subcultures. Norms also stem from the particular history of a given organization or group.

Norms are both created and enforced by all members of groups and organizations through conscious and unconscious behavior. The more conscious and attentive we are to the norms in groups and organizations, the more we can see which norms promote the goals of ourselves and the organization, and which frustrate them. Since norms are a major factor in determining organization climate, the extent to which the creation and enforcement of norms is a deliberate process influences the extent to which members of an organization can have control over their climate. As noted in earlier chapters, other factors affect internal organization climate, such as external conditions (e.g., the market), the organizational structure, systems, and written policies and procedures. All of these factors are subject to manipulation by members of the organization to some degree. But it is norms that have the strongest effect on the interpersonal, day-to-day climate, and it is norms that usually are the least-obvious factor because they tend to evolve unconsciously. Sometimes the evolution produces useful norms and sometimes it produces successive distortions that limit members to nonproductive rituals.

NOTES

1. William F. Whyte, *Street Corner Society* (Chicago: University of Chicago Press, 1943).
2. If you are interested in further reading in the area of norms, we recommend the following sources:
    Erving Goffman, *The Presentation of Self in Everyday Life* (Garden City, L.I.: Doubleday Anchor, 1959).

Jay Jackson, "Structural Characteristics of Norms," in B. Biddle and E. Thomas, eds., *Role Theory: Concepts and Research* (New York: Wiley, 1966).

Melville Dalton, *Men Who Manage* (New York: Wiley, 1959).

3. The control of output by informal group norms was one of the most powerful concepts generated by the classic Hawthorne experiments. See F. Roethlisberger and W. Dickson, *Management and the Worker* (Cambridge, Mass.: Harvard University Press, 1939).

4. The problems with sacred norms are enhanced by the fact that they can be manipulatively used (supported) by power-seeking individuals who have advantages to be gained from having areas of organizational functioning that are not open to influence by the general membership.

5. For an excellent description of how organizations create these traps and how individuals enforce the trap-rules on each other and themselves, see Sam Culbert, *The Organization Trap* (New York: Basic Books, 1974).

6. Alexander Solzhenitsyn, *The Gulag Archipelago* (New York: Harper & Row, 1973).

7. Chris Argyris, *Behind the Front Page* (San Francisco: Jossey-Bass, 1974), especially pp. 107–109 and 248–249.

Chapter 5

Analyzing
and Improving
Norms

In Chapter 4 we described some of the major ways in which
social norms create or influence the climate of an organization.
The natural next question is concerned with change or improvement: you understand how your norms are affecting the climate
in your system; how can you change them to be more what you
would like them to be? You may want to change the norms because you think the present climate is unhealthy or ineffective.
You may want to change them because you don't like the present
climate. Either motive is reason enough to explore the methods
you might use to effect these changes.

The following discussion proposes a variety of change
methods and includes some examples of their application in
particular organizational situations. The examples may or may
not fit your own situation, but they should suggest some ways
you can go about choosing methods.[1] For convenience, we have
grouped them under three general goals: (1) to *increase awareness* of the norms in your group or organization; (2) to *explore the
consequences* of the existing norms; and (3) to *take action* or
choose between existing norms, thereby controlling climate.

INCREASING AWARENESS

One of the first tasks in improving the norms of a system is
to be able to perceive what the norms actually are. In this area,
as in many relating to human behavior, groups are usually
tempted to jump to the process of evaluating and changing

norms before adequately describing them. The following activities have been used to help groups more clearly perceive the rules under which they operate. Most of them have been conducted with the help of a consultant of some sort, but this is not really a requirement. The only requirements are knowledge of the activity and a desire on the part of the members to become more conscious of the climate in which they live and work. If they are willing to explore this area, a number of activities can be useful.

Spotting Supernorms

One of the first efforts should be a discussion of "supernorms"—those norms that could interfere with the process of becoming more conscious of the climate, because they relate to behaviors that can hinder this process. Some obvious supernorms would be:

- " Don't talk openly about our norms."
- " Don't raise embarrassing topics."
- " Be polite at all times."
- " Don't be critical about the way things work here—it's disloyal."

For starters, someone has to be willing to take the risk of questioning these supernorms; otherwise, increasing awareness of norms will never get past the wishful-thinking stage. The group needs to be willing to suspend the more binding supernorms, at least for the purposes of an experiment, even though they may feel that in the long run these norms are useful and make it a more comfortable world in which to work. This is an instance of how critical it is to be committed to experimentation for purposes of *describing* what exists as a climate, with no implication of a firm commitment to change anything.

The Norm Census

The most basic approach to describing your group's norms (and the one we have used most frequently) is the Norm Census (NC). The purpose of the NC is literally to describe as fully as possible the norms under which the group is operating: What are the rules for the games being played? The emphasis is on identifying whatever rules exist, without prejudging whether they are good or bad, important or unimportant, exclusive to this group or imposed by the wider organization or society, and so on.

The NC has generally been used after an early consultation experience with a group. This introductory experience is useful primarily as a means for developing the group's ease and skills in perceiving and talking openly about *processes* that occur among members of the group. This helps to break down the resistance to norm analysis caused by the supernorms.

The steps in the Norm Census are briefly as follows:

Step 1. Before the NC: Obtain agreement from the group to perform an exploratory description of its norms, with no commitment to any particular outcome other than increased awareness of how group members interact.

Step 2. Decide on a time and place for the NC. A minimum of about 3½-4 hours is usually necessary for the NC so that urgency doesn't cause the process to be rushed and superficial. The place needs to be comfortable and have plenty of visual display materials, so that everything generated can be written down and easily seen by everyone. We have found that the NC tends to be more productive when held in the group's own spaces, rather than at some off-site location (such as a hotel or conference center), since the group's own setting provides numerous reminders about (and is a contributor to) the climate in which they work.

Step 3. Starting the NC: A brief orientation on the nature of norms and how they contribute to the climate and effectiveness of groups and organizations. In our own work, this has generally been an abbreviated form of the discussion of norms in Chapter 4. This orientation helps people to have a common definition of norms and what they are trying to do with the NC.

Step 4. Brainstorm (without being too precise) a master list of all the norms that affect the climate in the group. Again, the emphasis is placed on what *exists*, not on what is important or useful or good. We often split the group into two (random) subgroups and have each prepare a list, in order to minimize the impact of taboos or blind spots that may develop during the process of generating the list. Each subgroup tends to include those items that the other subgroup has avoided. This listing can take up to an hour or longer.

Step 5. Share lists (if done in two groups) and generally discuss the picture presented by the norms list: Are some items patterns rather than norms?; Are there splits within the group over whether certain norms really exist?; Do some norms only apply to certain people or situations?; and so on.

Step 6. Identify the consequences and impact the different norms (and the overall pattern) have on life in the group. Which norms facilitate what the group is trying to do, and which ones tend to inhibit? Which ones create an invigorating climate, and which ones tend to stifle? Which ones would be amenable to change, and which ones are more or less fixed?

Step 7. Select some particular norms for change, including the elimination of unwanted norms, alteration of the tolerance limits of others, and possibly the creation of new norms that are needed but missing at present. Some concrete goals should be set here, including who needs to change his or her behavior and when a follow-up session will be held to examine the progress that has been made. (Steps 6 and 7 will be explored more fully below in relation to "examining consequences" and "taking action.")

If you wish to obtain a final check on the extent to which people have been dealing openly during the NC, ask people at the end to write down anonymously any major norms they feel have not been touched on. These can then be shared immediately, if people are willing, or brought to the follow-up session to see whether these unmentioned norms may be blocking attempts to change the climate.

The Spaceman Game

When attempting to do a Norm Census, groups sometimes find they have difficulty visualizing their norms and describing them so that they can be listed. The Spaceman Game is a simple variation that helps to prime the pump for the Norm Census. It consists of asking members to imagine they are spacemen who have just dropped into the middle of the group and observed them in action without knowing what kind of beings they are and/or what they are trying to do. Knowing nothing, what would one's observations reveal about the point of their behavior and the rules that govern what they do?

Of course, it is not necessary to just imagine the spaceman process. The group can arrange to have an outside observer actually visit the group and observe them in action. (Or it could solicit reactions from an outsider who happens to be there anyway.) The observer can be a professional, such as a behavioral-science or management consultant, or a friend who is not so caught up in the group's systems that he or she cannot see the rules by which they are playing. Someone who lives in another climate is often a very good sensor of the particular norms that give the group its characteristic feel.

Individual Reactions

The first three activities have all been geared to a group-level diagnosis. Although norms and climate are social concepts, it is also possible to help individual members become more aware of the parts they play in maintaining the norm system and its impact on them. For those individuals who wish to learn more about themselves in this area, we ask them to spend an hour or more, at work, making notes on the following five questions about their life in the work group:

1. Which norms do I personally feel most strongly about in terms of them being important to our functioning as a group?

2. Which norms do I regularly help enforce when someone deviates from them?

"Different drummer my foot—he's never done anything right in his whole life."

3.   Which norms do I condone by tacitly agreeing—that is, by doing nothing when someone else makes an enforcement move on a deviator?
4.   Which norms do I personally dislike and/or feel stifled by?
5.   Which norms do I tend to deviate from, and what happens to me when I do? What would it take to change this into a nonnorm for our group?

After people answer these questions individually, we encourage them to test their answers with at least two other people in the group—preferably one who seems to live up to all the norms and another who seems to violate them regularly.

The Source Analysis

Another way of describing the normative system is to develop a picture of the sources of the various norms. Where did they come from—our own group, the organization, or the society as a whole? How did they develop historically, and what was their purpose?

We have not developed any particular exercises for increasing awareness in this area, but it has helped just to talk with the group about the history and sources of their norms. For instance, group members tend to develop different change strategies for dealing with norms that come from the group itself ("we can make the change ourselves"), from the larger organization ("if we change, we will have to either try to also change the organization's norm or hide our deviance from the rest of the system"), or from the society as a whole ("we will have to screen our activities so that they're not visible to outsiders"). The issue is how much control the group has over its own fate, and in what areas.

We have occasionally found that when a group conducts a source analysis they discover instances of pluralistic ignorance: they all adhere to a pattern of behavior they all dislike, but each believes that he or she is the only one who feels that way. The pattern seems to be a norm because no one has thought (or wanted) to take the risk of questioning it and where it came from. The source analysis can be a safer way of unlocking the more obvious instances of pluralistic ignorance with no further action being needed, since a shared dislike of the norm is revealed.

ASSESSING THE CONSEQUENCES OF THE NORM SYSTEM

We have been dealing primarily with efforts to describe the norms operating in the group and purposely trying to give this effort a chance by not confusing it with *evaluating* whether norms are good or bad. Now we would like to consider the assessment of the norms' impact (costs and gains) on group and organizational effectiveness and on the climate. We will not suggest specific exercises for this part, but ways of thinking which can help the assessment process be more systematic. Many of these ideas can be helpful to a group in the later steps of the Norm Census, when attempting to assess which norms are facilitative, which are inhibiting, and which missing norms are having an impact through their absence.

Effectiveness:
Assessing the Costs and Gains

The most basic question in evaluation is, What do we get (our gains) and give up (our costs) in return for using a particular norm as a control mechanism in this group? Take, for example, a norm that says, "We should not raise questions about the process of a group meeting unless we have a 'constructive' alternative to suggest." One client group generated the following list of consequences for this norm:

Gains
- The group's process can go on without a lot of interruptions.
- The leader is allowed to have a good bit of control over the process.
- People are encouraged to think of what we should be doing, not just what we shouldn't.
- We are less likely to be sidetracked.
- We can control a couple of members whom we don't trust to control themselves.

Costs
- The leader is allowed a good bit of control over the process.
- We are less likely to be sidetracked, even when we are headed down a wrong or a dead-end track.

• We spend a lot of energy and private attention trying to look constructive, even when we generally know that no one wants things to go badly (even the less-controlled members).

In this instance the group decided that on balance they paid a greater price (the inflexibility and difficulties in self-correcting) than they received in benefits from this norm. They decided that sensing that something is wrong can be a contribution in itself and that sharing this sense with the group allows everyone to contribute ideas about how to improve, without requiring that the "problem spotter" automatically also be the problem solver. They also agreed to deal with the self-control issue directly when a person was showing a pattern of excessive interruptions, rather than having an across-the-board rule which applied to every instance of questioning.

The most important step can often be simply the listing of the costs and gains a norm produces. A specialist in the behavioral sciences can be useful here for helping the group consider dimensions they are not normally conscious of, but the more practice a group has with this process, the less they need outside inputs.

Another strategy is to look for cases of successive distortion, as described in the previous chapter. A system needs to be able to recognize those norms that had positive functions when first formed, but which have gotten further and further away from their original purposes. Norms serving mainly symbolic or magical functions often carry considerably more costs in the present than the gains they provide.

When looking at the consequences of the normative system as a whole, it is useful to try to differentiate between behavioral areas that need a good deal of predictability and those that do not. Norms often apply to areas where wider ranges of behavior would make very little difference, but they represent a high price in "fallout" costs, such as increased rigidity, resentment of constraint, and encouragement to think uncreatively.

On the whole, we tend to think of the costs/gains analytic process as consisting of three components:

1. *Discrimination:* Identifying and/or weeding out those norms that are now costing us more than we get in return (or will in the future), without being blocked by the fact that they may have been worth it at some time in the past.

2. *Reconstruction:* Recommitting ourselves to those norms that seem to have a high payoff and relatively low cost; agreeing to enforce stronger sanctions if they are weak for these key norms.

3. *Generation:* Identifying areas where we pay a high price for not having norms that would make our behavior more consistently effective (such as a norm about getting to meetings on time and/or starting meetings on time regardless of who is there); then generating new norms predicted to have a high payoff.

Climate:
Assessing the Feel of the Place as Influenced by Its Norms

The second major question involving the consequences of norms has to do with how it feels to live with them. In our view, it is just as legitimate to question norms because they create an unpleasant climate as it is to question them because you think they are not effective. In the long run, a climate that people don't like will tend to drive out anyone who has alternatives available, and effectiveness will tend to drop as well.

We will not go into detail about this assessment, since this book is aimed at helping readers become more aware of the factors that influence the climate in their organizations and the consequences in terms of vitality, uses of energy, pleasure, and growth. These same dimensions can be a useful guide for beginning an assessment of the impact of specific norms or of the normative system as a whole.

ACTION AND CHOICE

The third general category of change activity, after expanding awareness and diagnosing consequences, is trying to actually change the norms and create new choices to be incorporated in the system. Since all of the activities discussed in this chapter have the potential to lead to change, this third category is not totally independent of the first two. However, the purpose of the following actions is more directly related to the goal of change, whereas the first two categories are aimed at creating a shared information base that can be used to set specific change goals.

Change goals should depend on your diagnosis, that is, on whether the climate is too stifling or too chaotic, too stormy or too placid, too unpleasant or too comfortable, or whatever.

Dropping the Past/Facing the Future

One fairly straightforward method for change is for a group to consciously decide which norms it wants to keep, which it wants to drop as past relics, and which new ones need to be added to meet future needs. This decision process has been done efficiently following the Norm Census and an analysis of costs and gains. Both of these steps are necessary in order that the members have a shared definition of the problems they are solving and recognize which norms are responsible. As a public activity, this group decision process also has the advantage of freeing people from constraints that were fantasies in their own minds rather than actual norms.

Declaring Experiments

If a group is not sure it wants to commit itself to a particular change of a norm, it may still be willing to take a first step, to experiment. This is just a decision to try a new behavioral pattern that violates an established norm, and thereby test whether the assumed results are really negative (as those who do not wish the norm changed have been arguing they would be).

The experiment should be relatively concrete in terms of spelling out which norms will be deviated from, to whom they apply, and how long the experimental period will last. At the end of this period, there should be a follow-up session to discuss the results and decide whether to make the changes permanent.[2]

Differentiation

Another useful change activity is for a group to work collectively on sharpening their norms so that they apply to necessary situations and do not spill over into unnecessary ones. One of the most stifling aspects of group norms is the organizational tendency to apply them across the board. An example would be rules of dress that are not tailored to vary with the person's activities, the physical weather, or changing moods.

Differentiation is also helpful in specifying to whom the norms should apply. If typical arrival and departure norms are fine for the bulk of employees but actively block the performance and morale of some subgroups, variations in the norm should be legitimized. This helps the subgroups feel like contributors, not traitors.

Similarly, the group may discover differences between norms in terms of the acceptable range of variations that can be allowed and still not interfere with system survival. Some norms, such as one against killing fellow employees, need to have narrow limits; other norms, such as how one arranges one's office space, allow people to choose within very broad guidelines with no loss in effectiveness and a gain in freedom of movement (psychological as well as physical).[3]

Enhancing Enforcement (Shaping-up Sanctions)

An important, but often overlooked, norms-change strategy is to improve the enforcement process, so that key central norms are effective in controlling members' behavior. In some instances, you can do this simply by being more explicit about the sanctions applicable to various kinds of deviance. Or, if sanctions are clear in theory but not carried out in practice, you would need to agree to a more rigorous enforcement procedure. Third, the sanctions may be clear but not very meaningful to the members, so that the actual cost of deviance is low. If the only price for arriving late at a meeting is some weak kidding (since the others have waited for you), you will probably tend to be late whenever some competing activity puts you in conflict. If the price for lateness is missing the first part of the meeting (and not participating in its decisions) and/or being excluded from future meetings of that group, there is a strong incentive to be there on time. This would hold true *if* you have commitment to that group's activities. If you don't, they are better off to get on with it whether you are there or not, and you are probably better off somewhere else.

Regular Review

If your group has started a process of examining and updating its norms, this process is likely to die out unless you can make it relatively simple for people to raise issues or questions about

"In the first place, Ms. Hinckly, the abolishment of the dress code applies to students only."

their norms as life goes on in the system. Doing it once, such as at a weekend workshop, does not really do the job, since the change process is likely to be a less-than-perfect, long-term affair. With this in mind, we would strongly recommend that a group wishing to improve its climate should be prepared to create some kind of forum or setting where it is legitimate for a person to talk about norms (positively and negatively) without acquiring the stigma of taking the group away from "real" work. A periodic climate, or norms, review session can serve this purpose. How often and how long the sessions should be would depend on your specific situation, but they probably won't have much impact if they are less than two to three hours per session and less frequent than once every three months or so.

Individual Deviance (Kamikaze Tactics)

All of the above activities and strategies implicitly assume some collaborative activity based on shared perceptions of the value of change. However, you may also have experienced situations where you believed you were the only person in the group who resented, rejected, or wanted to reshape a particular norm. In this case, your most straightforward action can be simply to deviate from the norm and live with the consequences.

This deviance can demonstrate that things do not fall apart when the norm is not followed. It can be a symbolic statement that says the price of conformity to that norm is too high—in terms of human dignity, your own effectiveness, the health of the system, or whatever. Deviance from a norm is often the only act that catches peoples' attention enough to generate a forum for dealing with the issues, as in the case of the draft-card burners who challenged the norm of acquiescence with induction into the United States forces fighting in Vietnam.

One outcome of deviance can be to get yourself punished and/or banished from the group. In order to use deviance as a tactic for change *and* survival in the system, you should try to clearly connect your act with the negative costs of the present norm (as you see them). In effect, you are trying to shift the deviant role you are playing:

from "public enemy" ⟶ to ⟶ "concerned citizen."

If you are successful, you also help to legitimize the questioning of norms as a demonstration of *concern* for the system and its people, rather than just a demonstration of personal instability or immaturity.

Acquiring an Ally

Even if your intentions are the best, you may still be perceived as a renegade who is upsetting an otherwise well-balanced system. You are much more likely to survive and have an impact if you have the support of one or more other people who have some legitimacy in the eyes of your group or organization. Sometimes the ally is most useful if he or she is an outsider to the system, such as a consultant. The outsider's expertise is often highly valued and his or her inputs are also more likely to be seen as unbiased — that is, not based on any particular career interests within the system which would motivate "power plays" (which is how your own deviance may be seen).

It is also useful to have an inside ally — someone who can at least support your right to raise the issue of whether the norms and climate are appropriate. They don't have to agree with you about changing a particular norm, but they do need to agree that the testing process is worthwhile. If you acquire an ally who is influential in the system, of high status, or an opinion leader, so much the better.

SOME CLOSING THOUGHTS

In the preceding sections, we have sampled a variety of activities aimed at awareness, diagnosis, and change of normative systems. We will close the chapter with some generalizations about two areas: the *threats* that tend to inhibit the change process, and the *necessary conditions* to facilitate change.

Threats

When trying to change a group's climate or process, you are always working against counterforces that generate resistance to the change. These forces often take the form of people feeling threatened by some sort of possible danger, negative outcome, or personal loss. We have observed several key threats in our work in changing norms:

- *Change threatens those people who feel responsible for the history of how the norms got the way they are today.* To change them now implies that a "mistake" was made, and that they made it, even though the norms may have been perfect for their time and only need changing because the people or conditions have changed.

- *Change threatens those people who "make out like bandits" under the present patterns.* This includes those who like the climate the way it is and those whose power is upheld and supported by the present norms. They tend to have a fixed-sum view of power — i.e., if others acquire more power over the group's processes, they will have lost power (versus the view that the group's total influence over its own fate can be increased).

- *Change threatens those people who fear that the group is brittle and will disintegrate unless all present norms are maintained as necessary integrating mechanisms.* This is the extreme of the "magical" function of norms, where even those norms that block good performance are considered sacred just because they already exist, even if they are, in fact, keeping the group split apart.

Our point here is not to engage in a lengthy analysis of forces that block normative change. We simply wish to alert the reader to the most common feelings of threat, so that they can be dealt with directly and not left as uninfluenceable factors. For example, if a case can clearly be made that changing norms does not equal finding culprits who made mistakes, then the strength of this threat can be reduced.

Necessary Conditions for Changing Your Norms

In the course of this chapter we have mentioned a number of necessary conditions or prerequisites for an effective normative change process to improve climate. Some of these have been stated, while others were merely implied by the kinds of activities suggested. These conditions can be thought of as positive forces helping to offset the threats described above.

Felt need for change: There is no substitute for the desire for things to change, for the creation of a better climate. If no one except yourself wants to improve the climate, you are probably always going to be fighting an uphill battle. If *you* don't even feel the need, really, but want to work on the norms because you feel you should, then our simplest suggestion would be to forget it.

Free discussion areas: In order to assess the nature of your group's norms and their impact, you have to relax the supernorm against discussing norms. You need to be able to discuss both specific norms and the whole process of how the norm system works in the group. If either of these are taboo topics, it is very difficult to set any change goals, since different people have different (unshareable) views of the problems and possible solutions.

A sense of concern: Our discussion is based on a major assumption that people will care about changing the norms, and that this caring will provide the energy to generate action. This caring about change, in turn, assumes that people have a sense of concern or caring for one another. When this concern exists, change can occur without everyone having to feel the same way about a problem. If you care about fellow group members and they feel that the climate is bad for the system and for themselves personally, you will contribute some energy to at least exploring the possibility of change. If you don't care about them, then that's their problem, unless you feel that the climate is not good for you. A mood of mutual concern allows exploration and testing to occur much sooner.

Support from power sources: Most change activities wither very quickly unless they are supported by people who can influence the attention and energy the system's members put into different activities. It is a great help to have support from influential members who can live with others' influences on the group's life, and who are secure enough not to feel overly threatened by the possibilities of new norms.

Appropriate settings: The details of day-to-day "business as usual" tend to drive out other kinds of issues, including the question of how effective our norms are. We do not think that a norms-change process will have a lasting impact unless the group creates some kind of setting where people don't feel they are diverting the group or wasting time when they bring up norm-related questions. Whether you use periodic norm-review sessions, weekend retreats to look at group process, or whatever, you need to design a setting that makes this type of discussion acceptable.

NOTES

1. The last chapter in this book deals more specifically with the problem of choosing appropriate change strategies.
2. If this follow-up session is not held, those who reluctantly agreed to experiment will be confirmed in their fear that an "experiment" becomes a fact once it has begun. This will make them even more wary of future experiments.
3. Sometimes the wrong differentiations are made. Many public schools have dropped strict dress codes after years of protest by students, then used this as an example of increased openness of the climate, with no actual change in the more controlling norms about low disclosure.

Chapter 6

Fear as a Special Climate

One particular climate worth considering specifically, because it is found so frequently in organizations, is the climate of *fear*. Many managers have theories or assumptions about fear as a useful motivator of behavior, and it therefore seems important to examine this special climate in order to describe what it can and cannot produce.

What do we mean by a climate of fear in relation to organizations? Basically, we are referring to a mood or climate that promotes within organization members (or some subgroup of them) the feeling that they are in danger of losing something, or of having some very undesirable event befall them if they do not "watch their steps." Essentially, they feel threatened in terms of their organizational existence or their future possibilities in the system. Their fear of loss may involve different things: loss of livelihood, loss of face, loss of self-esteem, loss of reputation, loss of opportunities for development or career progress, and so on. Whatever the specific concern, whenever a person feels that his or her life state in the system is in jeopardy, he or she is experiencing the fear we are talking about. When this fear is shared by many members of the group or organization, we can say with some assurance that it is not just an individual's timidity or sense of insecurity—it is instead a characteristic of the system's climate.

In terms of the weather analogy, a climate of fear is one in which people feel they have to wear "protective clothing" of various sorts in order to survive in an essentially hostile environment. Over a long period, the continuous wearing of heavy overcoats or rain gear can become burdensome: people get tired of carrying the extra weight and have less energy available for growth-producing activities. A climate of fear is, by definition, the one most likely to motivate people to put on their protective clothing. In practice, this can mean behavior ranging from not taking any chances in order to avoid making mistakes to hiding information that would anger or disappoint the boss.

SOURCES OF A CLIMATE OF FEAR

What causes this kind of continual bad weather in a system? Although the causes are many and varied, we can give at least a sense of them here. One source is the ways in which conflicts are resolved in the system. The greater the prevalence of resolutions based on power or persons getting "one-up" on others rather than joint problem solving, the more likely people are to think first about covering their flanks and avoiding being boxed-in.

A second source is the way career decisions are made. The greater the prevalence of a person's superiors deciding his or her organizational future without his or her involvement, the higher the price people perceive for doing things that might be evaluated negatively by those in control. This is particularly true if the organization is one where people get labelled early in their careers as "executive" and "nonexecutive" material.

The late Fred Allen described this source of anxiety very well:

Within the hierarchy of the little men there is no man who can outlittle the minor executive in a large corporation who treats his authority as he treats a tight suit. In a tight suit he is afraid to make a move. With his authority the minor executive takes the same precaution. There are thousands of these negative men huddled in the places where minor executives conceal themselves in the labyrinths of big corporations. They use the clam philosophy. If a clam never sticks its head out it is never overtaken by trouble. If a minor executive never commits himself he can never be cited for anything that has gone askew in the business.[1]

It is also interesting that Allen saw this pattern as a *personal* failing of these "little men," whereas we see it also as a phenomenon of the *social system*—i.e., there are settings where most people will behave as if they were wearing tight suits, even if they vary a great deal in their individual styles.

A third major factor is the general level of mutual trust in a system. If members see the system as basically a win-lose competition where people are concerned only with getting ahead, then fear will be high. This lack of trust arises from many different sources: intergroup competition; scarce resources and inadequate decision processes; low interpersonal competence, where people are not conscious of the conditions they create for one another[2]; and competition for scarce positions of advancement, usually coupled with a rigid norm about what "progress" should mean to a person in the system (up the pyramidal ladder). All of these can create mistrust, which in turn promotes the protective behaviors associated with fear or threat.

Jack Gibb, a behavioral scientist and consultant to organizations, nicely summarized the behaviors in groups that tend to lead either to supportive or defensive climates. In a defensive climate, one's first thought is self-preservation. The behaviors he suggests are as follows:[3]

Supportive Behaviors	Defensive Behaviors
Description	Evaluation
Problem solving	Control
Spontaneity	Strategy
Empathy	Neutrality
Equality	Superiority
Provisionalism	Certainty

In the left column are behaviors that tend to promote a climate of support (and hence more free behavior in others); in the right column are corresponding behaviors that create a threatening climate and thereby raise defenses in others. Evaluation is generally more threatening than description because people try to maintain a relatively positive self-image; evaluation, even though aimed at a piece of work, often implies evaluation of the person as well. Description involves describing behavior and its consequences concretely rather than simply labelling behavior as good or bad. This leaves the locus of control of the evaluation process within the person (and hence causes less defensiveness) rather than in the hands of someone else.

Similarly, a problem-solving stance toward an issue is likely to raise less fear and threat than is a stance of control, where the other person senses that your main interest is in controlling him or her rather than in solving the problem. This problem is especially apparent in many boss-subordinate relationships, for even though the boss may believe that he or she is working on the problem by controlling the subordinate, the subordinate seldom feels the same way. Often, focusing on control defeats problem solving, since this control is more apt to evoke self-protective behavior than efforts toward finding a solution.

Behavior perceived as "strategy" produces more defensive behavior than "spontaneity" for similar reasons. If you are perceived as having some preplanned interest in how a discussion is resolved and you are disclosing pieces of your plan in order to commit others to it in small steps, they are likely to trust you less and to want to see where the whole plan is leading. A strategy implies that the strategist does not trust what might be developed jointly, but rather must attempt to "win," which also implies that others might "lose" in the process.

A stance of empathy creates more of a climate of support than does neutrality, because one senses a willingness on the part of others to consider an individual's problem as *their* problem as well, and be willing to help find a solution. We have seen discussions about budgets and reorganizations go on interminably, each person defensively protecting his or her full territory, because each felt the others would consider it *his or her* problem if a particular change (good for the group as a whole) made it difficult for that person to fulfill responsibilities. A climate of empathy would have encouraged them to explore solutions not necessarily in their own immediate self-interest.

On almost any dimension, behaviors designed to demonstrate the superiority of one person over another will cause the second person to feel threatened and defensive. People need to perceive themselves as basically competent in their dealings with the world; to have another person promoting his or her own superiority poses an open-ended threat. That person may want to extend his or her prerogatives as a "superior" person into areas that others do not see as legitimate. Therefore, it is safer to avoid the superior-inferior definition to begin with, if possible. The works of Stephen Potter[4] are wonderful explorations of this jockeying for position where the climate is one that puts great emphasis on who is up and who is down.

Finally, provisionalism promotes a climate of support more than certainty does, because it does not imply that one person has a direct pipeline to truth or reality and that the whole point of discussion is simply for others to accept his or her revelation of the "truth." Argyris has called this kind of certainty a producer of a "norm of conformity" in a relationship, since it implies that people should accept one person's view of reality simply because he or she states it, not because they perceive it that way themselves[5].

Another factor that contributes substantially to fear-based climates in work organizations is the assumption held by many managers that it is useful and indeed necessary to use fear as a main motivator of human effort at work. This is the theory of motivation that Douglas McGregor labelled "Theory X" in *The Human Side of Enterprise* — the notion that people in general will not perform the work required for system performance unless they are motivated by fear (loss of job, pay, esteem, opportunities, etc.). Our experience in working with managers is that this is still a widely held assumption: managers generally believe that fear is the only motive one can really count on in a pinch.

Later in this chapter we will discuss what we believe you *actually* can count on fear to produce, and what you cannot, but it is interesting to speculate about why Theory X is such an appealing assumption to managers. Sometimes we have suspected that the process is self-sustaining: people who work in an organization with a climate of fear develop theories that help them accept this type of climate. The fact is that systems vary as to the general level of fear they create, but since many of the ones we have encountered tend to generate fear regularly, we think of this as "the way things are" altogether too often. Through this assumption, fear as a motivator can breed itself indefinitely unless the process is challenged openly.

In sum, people respond to a fear climate by putting on their protective clothes or by staying "inside" their own areas, which are relatively protected and warm. The conditions that generate fear in a system include: threats of harsh or uninfluenceable evaluations; unpredictability and uncertain commitments that may have a big negative impact sometime in the future on one's career; a feeling of lack of mastery over one's own fate as a human being, such as feeling that others are more interested in controlling one than in doing any particular task; and personal belief of theories that fear is the best motivator of subordinates' behavior.

CONSEQUENCES OF FEAR AS A CLIMATE

We must now ask some questions about the consequences of fear when it is a pervasive climate in an organization. These questions and their answers are meant to be illustrative, since much has been written about fear as a motive (although little about its system effects). It is important to consider both what fear produces and what it blocks in terms of human effort.

First, studies on both animals and humans have shown that fear can produce a state of arousal which, in turn, leads to action and performance of some task that is seen as likely to reduce the threat. This fits the managerial theory that connects threat with positive action, although several studies have indicated that punishment tends to suppress but not really eliminate unwanted behavior[6]. This is similar to Kelman's theory that coercion as a means of influence is inefficient, because it requires the presence of the coercer and his or her threat of force to maintain the desired behavior. In most cases no real attitude change has taken place.

As a motivator of behavior, then, fear can work, depending on how high the level of fear is and what is meant by "work." The arousal function of fear ("getting them off their tails") is commonly accepted in organizations and there is something to be said for it. The evidence is, however, that the effects are curvilinear. Low to moderate fear improves some performance through arousal, but higher levels of fear actually *decrease* performance through anxiety, regression to "safe" behaviors, and the like. Also, insecurity tends to block creative or innovative responses to problems.[7]

Fear tends to encourage more behavior oriented toward survival (like a hard winter) and relatively less behavior oriented toward productivity, growth, pleasure, and providing pleasure for others. What productivity does occur will be that which people perceive as obviously tied to their survival in the system, so that conventional definitions of productivity get a great deal of attention and innovative production areas are avoided.

The productivity that fear motivates is often useful only in the short run. The best examples of this occur when a powerful external threat is posed, such as in combat situations or in a variety of less-extreme situations that call for fast energetic action, such as airline hijackings or aircraft malfunction. The fear may be caused initially by some external stimulus (the sky-jacking), but that event stimulates internal fear in the person (pilot) and in the organization (airline). In these circumstances, fear is the only rational response and is a mobilizer of energy in the system as well. The efficient and productive behavior that fear motivates in cases of this sort is unusual for two reasons: most people in most organizations are not trained to react adaptively to crisis situations; and, such behavior cannot be sustained on a continuing basis over the long run.

Fear tends to promote patterned, routine, procedure-oriented responses. It is also likely that the threats must be continued and reinforced in order to keep this level of behavior going, and this requires constantly expending energy to keep fear alive in the climate. In fact, fear tends to have a costly impact on organisms in terms of creativity and innovation in general. It has been found that animals, under high-threat conditions, fall back (regress) to earlier behaviors that worked for them in threatening situations, even when these have little to do with the present threat. In human experiments, it has been found that rigidity in problem-solving situations is correlated with insecurity, and that as fear increases, conformity behavior increases.[8] Also, fear as a drive seems to have deteriorating side effects that other drives do not: increased internal tension, general anxiety, quickened fatigue and let-down, increased acidity, and so on. A group of researchers at the University of Michigan did an exceptional job of documenting these effects in work settings.[9]

What are the specific implications of these findings? The more pervasive the climate of fear for an organization, the less likely that system is to be proactive; that is, to initiate new activities, move into new areas, define problems in new ways, and so on. There is a felt risk involved in straying from behaviors or ways of thinking about problems that have worked in the past. This might be likened to a group of pioneers who have established a fort in a relatively unknown area. The greater their fear of the wild animals and other (real or imagined) threats outside the walls, the less likely they are to explore that new territory. They will tend instead to rely on stable, already-familiar life patterns to get them by.

Many organizations also have climates that promote staying within the walls of the fort. A norm may exist that it is better to do nothing than to make a "mistake" which goes on your record for the rest of your organizational life. In this atmosphere, a person who wanted to "stay alive" would see high risk in exploring new ideas and areas and relatively low payoff, and would be less likely to follow intentions, push for what he or she believes, or put energy into trying to develop truly new solutions to recurrent problems. In such a climate, people tend to overlook new directions that could define new roles for themselves, their groups, their organization. They and the system may be poor at sensing changes in the environment, since recognition of change could threaten or call into question the conventional picture they have agreed to call reality. Many of our bureaucracies are organizations with the kind of climate we have been describing in this chapter, where exploration and innovation are actively discouraged.

SYSTEM COSTS OF FEAR

Part of Maslow's theory of a hierarchy of needs suggests that the "need to know" and to grow in understanding is instinctive, but that it can be blocked by anxiety and fear of not surviving. On the other hand, security and lack of fear tend to encourage the expression of this need. This is why "training" situations that have a major emphasis on evaluation of the attendees for future jobs tend to produce little true learning or growth. The situation encourages *performance* of those things that the person knows he or she is good at, rather than forays into areas where real *learning* is possible. They tend *not* to innovate, to try to find new solutions, or to raise fundamental issues that could lead to new learning but which would require confrontation—possibly with the boss or others from whom they fear retaliation.

Another common consequence of fear climates is that those self-initiating types of people who find a coercive climate alien tend to seek out other, more-open climates, leaving behind those who "play it the company way," as in *How to Succeed in Business Without Really Trying.* (The dynamics of fear-inducing climates are by no means limited to business organizations; the civil service, religious institutions, the military, and universities are all susceptible.) This process can make it difficult for an organization to "grow" and keep the kind of executives it needs for leadership roles at the top of the system.

The more a system's climate encourages or demands self-protection above real production, problem solving, or growth, the less likely the system is to be flexible and adaptive to changing needs and conditions. If the general thrust of many writers' predictions is correct, it is becoming more and more important that organizations in any field be able to sense changes and develop new structures and processes for dealing with them.[10] A major cost of fear as a climate is that it tends to encourage *less* exploration and *more* regression to old solutions as stress increases; and stress is usually the companion of rapid change.

This cost to the health of the system shows itself in many forms: rigidity, inadequate information sharing, growth opportunities missed because "we can't allow anyone who is not completely experienced to handle this," loss of the more proactive people, control by people who have little access to the information necessary to exercise that control effectively, myths about "effective performance" which actually glorify mediocrity as an end in itself, mistrust between different parts of the system (and therefore lowered contact), and on and on.

If it is true that change is an increasingly normal aspect of organizational life, and we believe that it is, then these costs, which are both real and cumulative (they feed on one another), are key signs of an unhealthy organization, a system likely to destroy itself in the long run.

The use of fear as an influence strategy is partially a "maximin" strategy: an attempt to put the floor on the minimum energy that people will expend for the system. It is also partly a vicious circle: those who have grown up (organizationally) in such a climate assume that this is the way things are, have to be,

"Mr. Lamson blamed the loss of the Ranktox account on B.R., who traced the difficulty to the new sales manager, who pinpointed the problem in the Eastern Division, Ms. Hatch's area. She located the slip-up in Production, explaining as much to Frank Banes, who fired his secretary, who said she had a few details to clean up before she leaves."

and *should* be; each generation passes it on to the next. The un-intended consequence of both the maximin strategy and the "pass it on" phenomenon is that it tends to reduce the heights to which people may soar, since it puts a premium on not making a mistake or failing. It tends to lop off the top part of the curve—the peaks—while trying to smooth out the potential valleys (which the system says should be avoided).

Our view here is clear: it is nonfunctional for people to try to stimulate others by promoting a climate of fear in a group or organization. In every system there is enough natural fear of fail-ure, of unexpected changes in the environment, etc., for every-one to have a maximum useful level of anxiety. Adding more to this through planned *extra* threats is an unnecessary piling on, and in most cases tends to block rather than promote positive action.

A climate of fear will be unsatisfactory for anyone who wants to do more than put on woolen underwear and a crash hel-met each day and struggle back to where he or she stopped the day before. They will either try to change the climate, or will re-sign themselves to it and "exist" day-to-day in it, or leave it for a better climate. In the first case, the system may gain; in the latter two, it can become less and less adaptive to the world around it and more and more likely either to reach a crisis point or quietly slide into stagnation.

NOTES

1. Fred Allen, *Treadmill to Oblivion* (Boston: Atlantic/Little-Brown, 1954), pp. 210–11. Reprinted by permission of William Morris Agency, Inc. Copyright © 1954 by Fred Allen.

2. See Chris Argyris, "Explorations in Interpersonal Competence, I & II," *Journal of Applied Behavioral Science* **1**, nos. 1 and 3 (1965).

3. From Jack Gibb, "Defensive Communication", in *ETC: A Review of General Semantics* **22**, no. 2 (June 1965).

4. For an introduction to Potter that may change your life, see S. Potter, *The Theory and Practice of Gamesmanship* (London: Rupert Hart-Davis, 1947; reprinted by Penguin, 1962).

5. Chris Argyris, "Explorations in Interpersonal Competence, I & II," *Journal of Applied Behavioral Science* **1**, nos. 1 and 3 (1965).

6.   J. Appel and N. Peterson, "What's Wrong with Punishment?" *Journal of Criminal Law, Criminology, and Political Science* **56**, no. 4 (1965): 450-53.

7.   See H. Ainsworth, "Rigidity, Insecurity and Stress", *Journal of Abnormal and Social Psychology* **56** (1958): 67-74.

8.   John Darley, "Fear and Social Comparison as Determinants of Conformity Behavior," *Journal of Personality and Social Psychology* **4**, no. 1 (1966): 73-78.

9.   R. Kahn, D. Wolfe, R. Quinn, J. Snoek, and R. Rosenthal, *Organizational Stress* (New York: Wiley, 1964).

10.   For example, see Donald Schon, *Beyond the Stable State* (New York: Random House, 1971).

Chapter 7

Generating
a Climate
of Excitement

The opposite of a climate of fear is one of excitement. Such a climate has a strengthening effect on people, because they are challenged to stretch themselves and to develop in new areas. In this chapter, we will explore some of the characteristics of a climate of excitement and some ideas for generating one. Before reading our description, it might be useful for you to stop and write down your own list of characteristics to compare with ours. What makes an organization exciting for you?

We asked this same question of a group of business and government executives, and then discussed the factors they think contributed to peak experiences when they were particularly "turned on" in their work setting. They generated the following list of factors, which may or may not be similar to your own answers.

1. Pressure (time demands, restraints, physical danger)
2. Sense of achievement; meeting challenges
3. Recognition (from above; from peers; from subordinates)
4. Creativity; nonroutine personal contributions
5. New challenge
6. External forces (flood, riot, blizzard, etc.)
7. Continuing payoff: lasting consequences to actions
8. Unpredictability
9. Special phase in life of the organization
10. Anxiety and fear that things would not go well
11. Problem situations
12. High emotions

13. Nonpolitical decision making
14. High degree of personal contribution
15. Freedom to act
16. Feeling responsible (others dependent on you)
17. Significant consequences to your acts
18. Upward mobility—sense of change
19. Conflict
20. Personal satisfaction

CAUSES OF EXCITEMENT

One of the recurring themes noted in the above list is the degree of challenge in the system. People generally do not find an environment exciting unless they find it challenging. Some people can create challenges for themselves in an otherwise boring environment, but usually these are shortlived. We remember the student who reported that he managed to stay awake in a boring class by inventing new challenges for himself each day, such as predicting the number of times the professor would say "uh" in the course of his lecture, and then scientifically counting the occurrences. The environment must provide at least minimal challenges for those in it, and then people will begin to add additional challenges for themselves and others. In general, a sense of challenge is created by having difficult but achievable goals.

Another key contributor to a climate of excitement is the characteristic style of the system's leader. The more charismatic the leader is, the more he or she generates a climate of excitement.[1] Leaders have enormous influence in setting the organization's goals, norms, and informal rewards (strokes). Charismatic leaders are able to develop a "common vision" for the organization which both shapes and reflects the values held by the organization's members. Their own strength and ability has the effect of making others feel stronger and more able.

Some aspects of charisma are personality related; others are related more to one's philosophy and style of management. Vince Lombardi was a charismatic leader who generated excitement throughout the world of professional football, although his style was described as quite dictatorial. Other recent charismatic leaders whose styles differed from one another were John F. Kennedy, Charles deGaulle, and Martin Luther King. Each of these individuals was able to articulate a vision that captured the imagination of large numbers of people and generated a climate of excitement. In work organizations, it often is a strong leader who sets new directions and difficult but achievable goals.

Closely related to leadership is another cause of excitement: the diversity of people within the organization. Not only do outsiders tend to stereotype people in various professions and organizations (e.g., professors, FBI agents, musicians, business persons, clergymen, etc.), but often the people *within* the organizations subscribe to and reinforce the stereotypes themselves. This tends to damp out the diversity that naturally exists in any group. People believing in and living within a stereotype do not see (nor tolerate) many differences between themselves and others in the system. The organization or profession begins to attract a narrower range of people whose diverse talents and interests frequently aren't fully recognized. In our consulting work, we often observe such "undiscovered" abilities and gifts. Exciting climates are made exciting by having within them a wide diversity of people whose talents and skills can be fully utilized and appreciated.

Assuming that a system is full of challenge, has strong and dynamic leadership, and a mixture of good people, can it also be assumed that there will be a climate of excitement? We would answer, "Not necessarily." While the characteristics mentioned are the most important ingredients for such a climate, other factors can also have a causal effect. One of them is potential freedom of action. An organization's reward system must encourage the freedom to take risks—to try new things. People experience challenge and excitement when they are trying new things, and some people need to have this freedom to test themselves. Individuals often respond to extraordinary challenge with abilities even they did not know they possessed.

In most organizations these chances to test oneself are very rare because of the ever-present fear of failure. And yet the failure rate of people who get the chance is lower than one would expect. These opportunities usually occur in young and/or rapidly growing organizations characterized by tremendous challenges and a lack of trained and qualified personnel to respond to them. As a consequence, young and inexperienced people must grapple with situations "over their heads," and often they do very well indeed.

A classic example is the Peace Corps in its early days. President Kennedy inspired thousands of young people to volunteer their services to aid developing nations throughout the world. Many of the early volunteers (and their supervisors) had held no previous comparable positions and had no idea of what they would encounter in their host countries. A large number of people had extremely trying and challenging experiences which tested them to the limits of their capabilities. Almost all of those so tested and challenged showed remarkable stamina and inventiveness; when challenged, they "rose to the occasion." Similar examples occur whenever there are crisis situations. People challenged by the situation, the human need involved, the chance to test themselves, or whatever, manage to accomplish things they believed themselves incapable of.

Closely connected with the freedom to take risks is the freedom to fail. If the organization encourages people to take risks and then penalizes those who accept an extraordinary challenge and fail, it will quickly kill people's interest in accepting such challenges. If the price of failure is too high, the risk is not worth taking.

A less-objective aspect of exciting climates is the element of fun. If people are challenged, they are also likely to enjoy what they are doing and to exercise their senses of humor. In climates based on fear, humor is unnatural (except perhaps gallows humor) and may even be frowned on as frivolous or out of place. In a climate of excitement, humor is encouraged and is used by the leaders and other norm setters who realize it is a healthy ingredient in organization climate.

For us, it is generally more fun to work with people we enjoy, and this in turn generates an atmosphere of excitement. We do not believe in adages like, "Business and pleasure don't mix," or "Never do business with your friends." Most people, if given the opportunity to design their organizations or groups, choose individuals they like and trust. Although they may talk more about objective qualifications and relevant experience, the determining factor often is something much more subjective: Would I enjoy working with this person? Do I like and trust this person? In addition, most people are better able to resolve conflicts with those they like and trust than with others, and organizations relatively free of unresolved conflict are happier places to be. Organizations that pay *explicit* attention to the aspect of fun in the conduct of their work are more likely to have a climate of excitement.

We see interpersonal skills as the key to whether people who are friends can work well together. If the individuals can disclose both ideas and feelings to one another, if they can be open to new ideas, if they can support one another in risk taking, and if they can deal with conflicts and other issues early rather than let them fester indefinitely, then friends can capitalize on their bonds and be an effective team. If they do not have these skills, then the old adages are likely to prove accurate.

Finally, one characteristic that helps to differentiate exciting organizations from boring ones is the pace of events. As already noted, one cause of boredom is lack of challenge, a sense that "nothing's happening." People tend to feel more challenged (even by essentially boring tasks) when the pace of events is relatively rapid. Although studies have shown that merely increasing the speed of things will only alleviate boredom temporarily, a relatively challenging pace coupled with some amount of change (or unpredictability) helps to create an invigorating climate.

In terms of the four dimensions of climate we have used throughout the book, a climate of excitement has the following characteristics: a relatively *high amount of energy*; a fairly *wide distribution of energy*; a good degree of fun or *pleasure*; and a lot of *challenge that leads to growth*.

GENERATING EXCITEMENT

Now that we have explored some of the elements of a climate of excitement, the question becomes how to create such a climate. Many of the notions explored in Chapter 3 on changing the weather apply here as well, but there are some additional ideas we suggest you think about. First of all, whether you are a leader in the system or not, generating a climate of excitement can require considerable energy. This may be energy to overcome inertia in the system, energy to challenge and stimulate others, or energy to formulate and articulate a set of shared goals (e.g., a new mission or vision for the system and its members). In recent years, the principles and exercises of Gestalt Therapy have been applied to work organizations and have proved particularly useful for influencing the amount and kinds of energy in the system. Perceptual exercises, explorations of opposing points of view (versus trying to "resolve" them immediately), and legitimizing new sources of tension are some of the techniques that can increase system energy.

Secondly, generating new excitement almost certainly will require taking some significant risks, either for yourself or for the system, as do most steps toward greater self-determination by individuals and groups. This process helps to create what have been called "Origins"—people who feel they are generally masters of their own fate—as opposed to "Pawns"—people who feel that someone, or something else, is in control of their fate[2]. Challenging tasks, strong charismatic (but not totally dominating) leadership, and the freedom to test oneself by trying new things all lead people to feel that they are Origins rather than Pawns. Creating these elements in the climate is usually an uphill task.

Berlew[3] has identified five types of opportunities which can be sources of meaning and challenge in an organization:

A chance to be tested; to make it on one's own.

A social experiment; to combine work, family and play in some new way.

A chance to do something *well*.

A chance to do something *good* (for others, for society).

A chance to change the way things are.

Since these opportunities are scarce in many established organizations, people who are seeking this kind of chance for excitement tend to leave the organization to strike out on their own. "It is a mistake to assume that individuals who desert or reject established organizations are basically loners. In fact, many start or join new organizations, often at considerable personal sacrifice in terms of income, security, and working conditions."[4] Therefore, it is safe to assume that if established organizations could or would provide varied opportunities, these people would tend to stay with the organization. But to the extent that the organization makes people feel like Pawns, those most capable of helping to create or maintain excitement will leave the system.

Just such a phenomenon is occurring in public bureaucracies; those most capable of charismatic leadership either leave the system or are not attracted to it in the first place because of the enormous constraints in the environment. As a result, we see increasing numbers of articles in the press asking, "Where are our heros?" and "Why don't we have inspiring leaders today?"

To create excitement in an established organization, risks must be taken by those in power to allow others the necessary freedom to become Origins, and risks must be taken by those who want to become Origins in order to seek and accept the challenges and opportunities that will stretch them fully. The process is a two-way street requiring commitment for change from both sides. The need for such change is increasingly obvious from the expanding demands for worker participation throughout the industrialized nations of the world. It is a clear message from Pawns that they want to become Origins. If those in power cannot invent collaborative ways to help people be more in control of their own fate, it will be legislated or arbitrated through adversary relationships. It seems to us that, most often, such power-sharing solutions imposed from the outside do little to help people feel more like Origins and even less to change the climate toward more excitement. The spark of fun and challenge can be long gone from a system by the time adversary relationships have set in.

When discussing the causes of low-excitement climates, we mentioned the unexplored diversity of people within the organization. This view suggests a change strategy: *legitimizing* peoples' expression of different sides of themselves, rather than encouraging and rewarding the stereotyped behavior they often feel is the only "right" way to behave. Leaders should encourage members to use the skills and interest that are most alive for them, not the ones that look like everyone else's attributes, both within and outside of the system. This encouragement could be communicated concretely by suggesting that people take sabbaticals or retrain (inside or outside company training programs) as their special enthusiasms change over time.

Excitement is also created by working together toward shared goals—a mutually developed vision for the organization. Clear, agreed-on measurements for those goals should be estab-

"All I said was that this was an exciting climate to work in, where people take risks and feel challenged, but don't have too big a fear of failure."

lished so that people get concrete feedback on their progress. Ideally, the measurements are self-administered rather than carried out by someone higher up on the organizational ladder. Excitement is maintained by the pleasure derived from activities in the organization and the relationships between people; consequently, there is general motivation to do a good job.

A self-perpetuating cycle can be created when people have clear goals, good feedback on progress toward those goals, high motivation, and fun. These elements lead naturally to the establishment of more challenging goals and further excitement. A good example is a winning sports team. The intial goal might be finishing the season with more wins than losses (difficult, but achievable). As the team works toward that goal and has (for example) a string of three consecutive wins, the motivation to do a better job goes up and the goal gets changed to a more challenging (but also more risky) one, such as winning 70 percent of the games. A kind of synergism develops which allows each member's talents to be stretched. True interdependence exists and the team's fate rests on how well it works.

Interdependence in work teams can be similarly effective. The teams are usually made up of a number of functional specialists who are brought together to work on a mutual problem. Those teams that function in an interdependent manner can make fuller utilization of their total resources. Teams that want to learn to operate in this manner can profit from the help of an outside consultant (a coach, in the sports analogy of the previous paragraph). The consultant can serve as a role model for team members in the areas of trust building, relationship development, and interpersonal confrontation. Honest, straightforward confrontation without hostility can do more than any other single step to help team members learn to see one another as resources, broadly rather than narrowly. The external consultant can also be useful in that he or she can break the team's norms without being punished. That is, the consultant can introduce new forms of interpersonal behavior which are not part of the team's established game routine. As the consultant teaches the team members how to use him or her as a resource person, the consultant is by implication also teaching them how to use one another as resources. A climate of excitement is a by-product of the team-building process.

Keeping the climate exciting takes energy and commitment from all team members. They need to set new goals, push one another to achieve them, and develop some competition with other teams in order to keep spirits up. The aerospace industry abounds with illustrations of teams that achieved difficult technical tasks in record time because of the sense of excitement they had. During the Apollo program, many of these teams experienced the excitement of working on something of national importance against a timetable—getting a man on the moon by 1970. In addition, teams from different companies were competing with one another for the final NASA contracts. All these factors, internal and external, helped to keep alive a strong sense of excitement for many of the teams involved.

Within industry, parallel teams are sometimes given essentially the same task in order to generate competition between them as well as a climate of excitement. Where this is not possible, excitement can be generated by keeping a single team as informed as possible about progress being made on similar tasks in competing companies. Nothing builds excitement for a team as effectively as a good competitive race for a new product or market.

Excitement can also be generated by a threat. While a threat can easily be a source of fear and consequent protective behavior, it sometimes can get the adrenalin flowing and cause a lack luster team to begin to pull together in an excited and energetic way. One example we know of occurred at a college where the football team had been having losing seasons for several years, attendance had fallen off at games, and the administration was considering dropping the football program entirely. When this news became known on campus, the students rallied behind the team and the team caught the renewed sense of energy and purpose. They actually started to win games. The threat of elimination generated significant new energy and excitement for the team to cause a reversal of their performance.

Finally, excitement can be generated within work teams by a process of synergism—people sparking and energizing one another. Being in a work team with others one likes and respects helps to create a climate of excitement. Therefore, care should be taken when setting up work teams to choose members who are compatible with one another in terms of complementary skills, work styles, and personalities. A well-known example of a team matched according to these criteria was the astronaut group in the space program. While all teams can't be as carefully selected and trained together, certainly some additional attention to the areas of selection, compatibility, and training could help insure greater team excitement.

NOTES

1. A more thorough discussion of the connection between charismatic leadership and excitement can be found in an article by David E. Berlew, "Leadership and Organizational Excitement," *California Management Review,* Winter 1974, pp. 21–30.

2. Richard deCharms, *Personal Causation* (New York: Academic Press, 1968); and Richard deCharms, "Origins, Pawns, and Educational Practice," in G.S. Lessor, ed., *Psychology and the Educational Process* (Glenview, Ill.: Scott, Foresman, 1969).

3. David E. Berlew, "Leadership and Organizational Excitement," *California Management Review,* Winter 1974, pp. 21–30.

4. Ibid., p. 24.

Chapter 8

Climate and the Physical Setting

All human systems develop physical shapes and settings as they function over time, and these settings are tangible, concrete (as opposed to abstract) entities; they can be touched, seen, smelled, listened to, and so on. It is this quality of immediacy that makes the physical setting such an important aspect of organization climate.

In this chapter we will focus on two main topics: (1) the organization's physical settings as *indicators* or *reflections* of the climate of the organization, and (2) the physical settings as a *cause* of or *influence* on organization climate. These two views will be discussed both generally and in relation to the four weather dimensions used throughout the book.

SETTINGS AS REFLECTIONS OF CLIMATE: THE "FEEL" OF A PLACE

We all use the physical appearance of an organization's place of operation as a source of data about what that system and the people in it are like. Sometimes this is a conscious evaluation process, sometimes preconscious, where our "feel" for the place builds up without any specific awareness that our observations are changing our impressions of the organization. But whether consciously or not, we still use an organization's physical setting to make judgments about what it is like and what it would feel like to work there.

We get many kinds of data from these observations. We can tell something (with appropriate qualifications) about value systems, personal styles, decision processes, and even the history of the enterprise from the physical cues in the present. For our purposes here, we do not intend to explore all these aspects, but rather to focus mainly on physical cues as indicators of the nature and impact of the social-system climate on the people who work in it. None of the examples we use are meant to be immutable laws; they are indicators that we have found, on the average, to be useful as hints about certain qualities of the climate. Any single indicator, by itself, can only be suggestive, and must be tested against other information about the system.

In discussing physical settings as indicators of climate, we will consider increasingly specific attributes of the system: geographic location, overall exterior structure, and interior features.

Location

The first piece of information we get about an organization is its geographic location. Being in midtown Manhattan (New York City), in downtown Manhattan (Kansas), or in a posh, well-groomed industrial park communicates different messages about organization climate, values, and identity than does a location in an older, run-down part of a decaying urban area. In terms of the weather itself, a location in Connecticut is likely to have a different work pace than one in Alabama—due both to cultural differences and the physical climate in which the employees work and relax. Electronics firms in Southern California have a different feel and a more relaxed pattern of life than do the same kinds of firms in the Boston area.

Exterior Structure

The next impression we receive about a system, after knowing its location, is prompted by the actual building, workshop, factory, or whatever that defines and encloses the organization's spaces. The features of external facade play a large role in shaping our initial impression. Many companies today strive to project an image of progressiveness, solidarity, and reliability by building up-to-date but solid structures that look like other new office buildings. Contrast this with one job-hunter's first impression of his possible new employer:

> In the midst of the other yards I found one, no more than sixty feet wide, that was more strewn than the others with assorted junk: old wheel hubs, a dead truck or two, rusted garbage bins, cinder blocks, plastic barrels, and throw-away bottles and cans. At the rear of the yard was a decrepit garage. The mailbox out front told me this was the right place. It said, 'Liberty Refuse Co.,' in crude but clear letters. Some of the garbage trucks in the yard were lettered with 'Roberts Refuse Inc.' but the mailbox was surely closer to the facts. After all, it was a postal employee who got me here after all. The yard, the trucks, and the garage were certainly not what I had in mind when I read the imposing company name in the ad. But I was now in the yard and I wasn't about to run.[1]

Messages about climate can be difficult to read from the exterior, however, and cannot necessarily be taken at face value. A smooth, ultramodern exterior for a company's headquarters may represent successful, bustling vitality; or as C. Northcote Parkinson pointed out, it can herald a system in the advanced stages of decline, trying to look like its past vital self:

> A study and comparison of these [buildings perfect for their purpose] has tended to prove that perfection of planning is a symptom of decay. During a period of exciting discovery or progress there is no time to plan the perfect headquarters. The time for that comes later, when all the important work has been done. Perfection, we know, is finality; and finality is death.[2]

Conversely, headquarters in a run-down old building may say that the system lacks class and the energy to develop resources appropriate to their tasks; but it may also indicate an experimental organization that has a good distribution of energy and places little value on using external images just to keep up with those systems around them that are trying to *look* vital.

The clearest conclusion that can be drawn from the external structure of the system is simply that it represents choices that have been made by those in power. This image gives one an initial feel, or hypothesis, about what the system is like, which then can be checked against other data gleaned inside.

Sometimes judgments can be made about climate from the way the system's structure *relates* to its location. For example, the windowless school building may be technologically very interesting, but it also sends a symbolic message to its users, the teachers and the children. The message is that school activities have little or nothing to do with the surrounding world and the two should not intrude on one another. The opposite message (and climate) is fostered by decisions not to have any formal school building at all, such as with Philadelphia's "Parkway" high-school concept. In this case, the community is considered to be the learning setting, not an individual school building, and children go to different locations to meet different learning goals. Our hypothesis would be that the more sealed-off a school building is from its surroundings, the less likely the school is to promote growth in understanding the connections between learning and everyday life.

In sum, the exterior structure of an organization is one important reflection of the climate of that system, and its primary importance is that it is the first concrete experience a visitor has with the system. The exterior may or may not be an accurate reflection of what the system feels like to those who work there, but it establishes expectations in the visitor's mind (and often in the members' minds, too) when they arrive at the location. These expectations help determine what a person selectively perceives from the range of available observations that can be made about what the organization is like. Likewise, prospective employees use physical image as a criterion for choosing between employers when other factors are more or less equal.

Interior Features

For the richest visual picture of the climate of an organization, we must, of course, explore the interior spaces of the system. The way in which organization members shape and reshape their offices, production areas, and passageways provides us with most of our data about the social climate in which they operate.

For example, we are sure that most readers have at some time visited two organizations within a short period of time and been struck by the differences in appearance, in "feel" of the places, and in their reactions to them. Or, you may have changed jobs and noticed the contrasts when comparing the new setting with the old setting. Sometimes the difference is in the colors that have been used: one has a uniform painting scheme in "institutional" lime greens and pale pinks, while the other exhibits more varied colors, stronger hues, and patterns that vary from area to area within the total setting. The former tends to give the feeling of blandness and sameness, and like a constant geographical climate, this sameness can be tiring after a period of time. A uniform setting therefore may be indicative of low energy in the system's members and groups. The second setting symbolizes a valuing of differences, a range of choice about the feel of different areas, and a preference for expressiveness rather than simple conformity to one standard. Even if the combinations are not particularly elegant in aesthetic terms, their variety indicates that the climate allows different tastes and styles to flourish.

Another way of describing this feel is the extent to which signs of human habitation are present. Many work areas lack these signs: they are designed to be kept in their original untouched condition. Nothing should be placed on walls; desks and tables should not be moved, and so on. This fixed quality can exist in a well-established place, or in a new building where the money and time put into an "integrated" design create a strong vested interest in keeping things fixed. The integration is usually an advantage for the designer and the executive who made the budget decisions, but it may be a disadvantage for the actual users of the setting. At any rate, the effect on an observer of no traces of the people who are using the setting (things *they* have done to the place) is to give the feeling of being in a nonhuman system; the people as individuals might as well not have been there for all the difference they have made.

CLUES ABOUT THE CLIMATE DIMENSIONS

To return to the climate criteria we are examining in this book, what cues can we use from the organization's settings to make inferences about the amount of energy, the distribution of energy, the pleasure, and the growth potential for members of the organization?

Amount of Energy

One visual indicator of the energy in the system is simply the pattern of movement that is visible. Although it is not conclusive by itself, a visually inactive setting, with little movement, no changes in sound patterns, and the like, is often an indicator of a social system with a low energy level.

A second indicator of low energy is the continued existence of disruptive details in the setting. A coat rack left in the wrong place despite the inconvenience; a draft under a door that is neutralized by adding clothing rather than changing the physical structure that created the draft; the disruptive noises from the hallway that are tolerated rather than shutting the door—all of these may indicate a low general energy level for problem identification and problem solving. The theme is, "Well, we could fix that, but it's just too much trouble." This is the physical setting equivalent of that famous low-energy rallying cry, "Tomorrow we've got to get organized. . . ."

Distribution of Energy

What can physical-setting observations tell us about how energy gets distributed and used in an organization? One indicator is the extent to which security and separateness have been emphasized in the layout of offices and desks. The more that people have arranged to protect themselves from others, regardless of the need for connection or separation which their tasks require, the more the social climate is likely to be a harsh one, where survival in the system is a stronger concern than production or growth. Energy is likely to be focused on protection in social behavior as well as in structuring physical settings.

A setting where tremendous attention has been paid to all design details may represent a misdistribution of energy. Great attention is sometimes paid to physical detail as a means of avoiding fundamental task or power conflicts that people fear cannot be solved. In this sense, if the settings are *too* good, too well developed, we wonder about displacement of energy from central to more peripheral concerns. (See Parkinson's comment earlier in this chapter.)

In a related vein, the use of status symbols (size of office, privacy of work place, carpets, size and quality of desk, location, access to a window, etc.) can tell us a good deal about how energy is being used in the system. Every organization has some sort of symbolic language that relates physical features to the status of users in the system. What we look for, however, is the degree of emphasis on status itself and the degree of perfection of the status-symbol language. The more emphasis there is on each person having just the right trappings, the stronger the indication that a great deal of the system's energy is being channeled into unproductive internal scrambling for position.

The best example that we have discovered of energy being channeled into relatively useless symbol maintenance was the case of "musical chairs in the parking lot," so named by the employees of one company. It seems that in the parking lot the twenty or so spaces closest to the entrance were labelled with the name of their "owners," and of course closeness to the door was directly correlated with formal status in the organization. This meant that every time there was a promotion or resignation, with subsequent changes all down the line, each person affected moved up a space in the lot and corresponding names had to be repainted on the curb. One might ask why they did not have signs on sticks that could just be pulled up and set down again, but perhaps that would have been too graphic a signal of how transient everyone there was.

Pleasure

The extent to which the system is enjoyable to be in may be one of the easiest dimensions to interpret from the physical-setting cues of the organization. Our experience in organizational diagnosis and consulting strongly indicates that a place that looks colorless, drab, and lifeless often feels that way to everyday users, too. Sterile, identical corridors, uniform office spaces, stereotyped handling of such things as desk arrangements and who gets which locations—all of these imply a lack of excitement that reflects more than just how the physical place is structured.

Conversely, we believe that a setting which communicates a sense of joy, of personal markings, and of fun in influencing the setting indicates how the users feel about the social system as a whole. Personal posters, switching of desks, shared visual jokes—all of these help create a mood that reflects positive enthusiasm for being where the members are during their working hours. How people use their spaces can also indicate this pleasure, particularly if people tend to stay around the organization's spaces when they have the option of remaining or going somewhere else. The more work spaces are used as community gathering places, the more pleasurable we assume the climate to be.

Our last physical indicator of the pleasure members get from a system is how they treat their settings: the extent to which physical facilities are cared for or destroyed. Destructive behavior toward facilities often correlates with a lack of pleasure with the social system, or out-and-out alienation, although it can be compounded if there is dissatisfaction with the facilities themselves. We have been involved in several projects where social and physical system changes were made together, and one outcome of these kinds of projects is usually greater care on the part of members in using their new facilities.[3]

Growth

The main feature of physical settings as indicators of a growth climate is the extent to which they have had observable alterations or problem-solving done to them. As with several of the other dimensions, the extent to which people alter their settings is a clue to the potential for growth the climate holds. No signs of personal alterations may mean that people do not want to experiment with their surroundings; or, that norms or rules of the system actively prohibit tinkering, adjusting, and otherwise making a place one's own. In either case, the net effect is a climate where experimentation and feedback about results are not valued in the physical setting; and the likelihood is that this nonvaluing carries over into task- and social-interaction areas as well. It usually indicates a general inclination to go with well-proved rules and ways of doing things and a low priority for growth as a process.

For those who would like to develop further their skills of perception in this area, we recommend Chapter 1 of a book on organizational behavior by Coffey, Athos, and Reynolds[4]. As an excellent exercise in making inferences about systems from their physical settings, they present a set of matching photos from two companies with contrasting climates or "personalities".

"Yes, I suppose the decor *is* a bit unusual, but it has always seemed right to me."

SETTINGS AS CAUSES OF CLIMATE:
THE INFLUENCE PROCESS

Organizational settings are not only indicators of climate, they can influence climate as well. Some of our examples will overlap with the discussion of settings as indicators, since the separation into two categories is not nearly so neat in practice. For example, a color scheme that reflects conformity decisions made in the past because of a survival climate reinforces that climate in the present and future: people working there are always visually reminded of the pressures to conform.

First, some general points about the influence of physical settings on the climate. How do settings influence the feel of a place? A friend recently described to us two sections of a course in social psychology, both taught by him. One section met in the daytime, in a classroom with bright lighting, tile floors, and traditional bolted-down desks. The second section met at night, in one of the school lounges, with comfortable movable furniture and variable lighting. Needless to say, the two sections, although ostensibly studying the same thing, developed very different climates for doing so. In particular, our friend noted that the lounge section moved things around more, had more cohesion as a group, and talked about their own experiences and feelings as examples of the psychological processes they were studying. In the first group very few of these things occurred.

This simple contrast illustrates the power of the physical setting to influence the mood of people who use it. Each culture attaches meanings to various attributes of settings, and these meanings contribute to the expectations and motivations of those who use the settings. In the above example, soft lighting suggests more intimacy than harsh light; lounge-type seating suggests a more informal role relationship than does classroom-structured seating; the lounge arrangement suggests tinkerings and adjustments to suit the activity, while the classroom implies that the structure is right for classes, period. All of these are expectations about what "ought" to happen in a particular kind of place, just as we have expectations about how people ought to behave in a church or a discotheque.

Settings influence mood through the memories they stir up in people. An executive group that recently moved its headquarters into an elegant old mansion reports that members are delighted with it, and one of the best features is the extent to which the mansion stirs up memories of past experiences and eras. These kinds of associations are very different from those they had when they were headquartered in a cinderblock commercial office building with steel office furniture and no ornamental flourishes.

A setting can also influence mood through peoples' memories of past events in that setting itself. For instance, a room that is always used by an executive to chew out subordinates will have a very definite climate for them because of their memories of uncomfortable experiences there, even though they are presently in the room for an entirely different type of meeting. This effect is often used in literature as a plot vehicle: a magnificent old house becomes uninhabitable by its present owner after a loved one dies there. The place has a strong negative climate for him or her, even though outsiders may consider it a very desirable home.

Settings also influence climate through the activities that they facilitate or inhibit. The lack of a large enough meeting room to get a whole group together will deter the development of a sense of community in that group. An area that has all work benches fixed will encourage continuation of old activities, even when they are no longer particularly profitable or there is a better way to do the same tasks. A setting that allows noise or visual distractions, with no way of shutting them out, can promote a climate of excitement and vitality but at the same time be negative for tasks that require concentration and uninterrupted sequences of activities.

Rather than stop with only general examples, we will use the four climate dimensions as a means of describing some specific effects of the physical setting.

Amount of Energy

One factor that determines energy is obviously the geographical location of the organization and the accompanying meteorological climate. Organizations in Mississippi have different energy levels than ones in Illinois, on the average, although more and more systems are trying to reduce this effect through climate-control technology, which creates an internal setting that is constant and supposedly optimal for energy stimulation. Problems with this control arise, of course, when activities within an area vary as to amount of physical movement and when individuals differ in terms of their own optimal temperature and humidity. We have also seen problems with immediate climate control, such as the temperature of a meeting room becoming too high, leading to the quick deenergizing of a group. Such meetings are doomed to peter out unproductively unless those assembled recognize that their sluggishness is being caused by the setting, not the topic (although there are certainly cases where it *is* the topic).

Another physical block to energy is wrong-sized spaces for work. People bring potential energy to an organization, but unless there is some way and place to use it, the energy cannot really be considered available to the system. Scarce facilities, such as tools that people wait for or meeting rooms that can only be used by months-in-advance scheduling, tend to reduce the available energy of the system, too. One designer of office settings, Robert Propst, has used changeability as a key criterion for his systems, so that the user can adjust his or her setting appropriately for changing task needs[5].

Settings that reduce peoples' awareness of one another, such as having each person walled-off from every other person, can also contribute to a low-energy climate. Combinations of individual resources provide more effective energy for system tasks than would be expected from just taking the sum of the individuals available. A task force of four people can, if competent, do more than four times as much as the four individuals could do separately. Arrangements that allow people to see one another as they work and come and go from work tend to increase mutual awareness, encourage a sense of community, and stimulate thoughts of joint efforts. This is the other side of the privacy issue—if people are too sealed off from each other, it is hard for them to have a sense of where they fit into the total effort or an idea of what others are doing or could do for them.

Distribution of Energy

Settings influence the distribution of energy in many ways. For example, arrangements that require the same unchangeable space to be used sequentially for several different events can dissipate a great deal of energy in unproductive clean-up and set-up operations. This can be a problem for systems ranging from the creative-marketing area of a consumer-products company to an elementary school with strong policies against the children leaving their materials lying around.

More generally, physical facilities that are readily available encourage an efficient use of members' time on the job. Spatial arrangements that have slack in them, so that people can get together for meetings on very short notice, will tend to be more efficient for the human system than settings with very few meeting areas that must be scheduled far in advance. Unfortunately, facilities managers or planners tend to see efficiency only in terms of the percentage utilization of a space, rather than the percentage of effective utilization of people's time. Several highly paid managers having to delay a crisis decision due to no available meeting space can cost the system more than it saved over five years due to maintaining minimal ("efficient") meeting facilities.

Spatial arrangements with locational problems also decrease the effective distribution of energy. One firm we studied had their headquarters divided for a time into two locations twenty-six miles apart. It took a tremendous amount of energy just to keep the parts in touch with one another, let alone to do anything productive. This is an extreme example of the same problem two task-force members face when they are supposed to work as a team, yet have offices in widely separated areas of their building.

Facilities that are administered or structured so as to promote a competitive climate around scarce resources may have a high-use index for the facilities but generate a hidden cost through the side effects: decreased collaboration, fudging of need and use figures, increased mistrust, and decreased sharing of information. Settings often promote other costly internal competitions through their symbolic messages as well: barrier-like separations between the spaces for different groups, gauntlets of rejecting secretaries that a visitor must pass in order to penetrate a group's spaces, and other arrangements that highlight the differences between groups rather than their common goals or problems.

Our discussion at the beginning of this chapter touched on a setting's influence on mood, through the memories and fantasies it triggers in users. This influence can be a force for good or bad distribution of energy, depending on the appropriateness of the mood for the goals of the users. The training-center room that was also the scene of past evaluations of subordinates by top management will tend to trigger survival behaviors rather than risk-taking experiments for learning purposes, even when the ostensible goal is training and development. The atmosphere of the room itself encourages participants in the program to worry first about their image and second about whether they will learn.

Pleasure

The degree to which an organization's climate is pleasurable to its members is influenced by physical settings in some well-recognized ways. Areas that are aesthetically pleasing will be more enjoyable to work in, and the experienced pleasure from being at work will be higher. Several studies of changes in office facilities have found that members described themselves as enjoying the new place more than the old and looked forward more to going to work. Related to this feeling was a lowered turnover and absenteeism rate, and the above-mentioned tendency for people to take better care of their improved facilities than they did of the old. Perhaps this last tendency is partly due to the fact that it simply makes more sense to preserve something good, but it also seems logical that improved feelings of wellbeing motivate people to care about their surroundings.

Pleasure, by definition, is an individual phenomenon, determined by individual preferences. The kind of setting that one person enjoys (say, a lively, stimulating one with changing patterns of people coming and going) may be the cause of indifference or anxiety in another individual who prefers a placid, predictable setting with controlled stimulation. Since pleasure cannot occur independent of the person, it is also usually related to the degree of self-control a person has over the setting he or she is in. When people can influence their immediate surroundings and when they have some degree of self-awareness, they are more likely to shape their settings so as to make them pleasurable.[6]

Some general statements can be made about pleasure and settings, however. Some work organizations are involved in physical activities that generate noxious stimuli—noise, rancid smells, dust, intense heat or cold—which must be compensated for in some way in order that the workers not dread just being on the job. Other systems do not have particularly noxious processes to overcome, but even without this handicap, they still manage to create environments that are negative for most of their members. The usual features of these settings are blandness, uniformity that even the dullest individual finds boring, and the treatment of facilities as necessary evils not deserving of any real thought or creativity.

Members may become so resigned to uninteresting, non-involving work settings that they take them for granted, feeling that this is just the way things have to be in organizational life. In this sense, the setting is not a great source of displeasure for its users, but neither is it a source of positive excitement or enjoyment. We believe that an invigorating organization climate requires more than simply an absence of displeasure, and that by definition it contains sources of positive enjoyment both in the physical setting and in other, more socially oriented areas.

Finally, organizations' settings are helped or limited on the pleasure dimension through their geographic location. A plant located in upstate Vermont has a bit of a headstart on a similar plant in the New Jersey industrial strip, no matter what the design of the plant itself. Natural features and the prevailing weather are obviously factors in the enjoyment of a setting, and most organizations consider this when they choose a particular location.

Growth

In this society, people are not very accustomed to thinking of the physical environment as a source of stimulation toward growth. It is recognized as important in early childhood development, but most people have lost sight of the ways in which interaction with the environment can be a continuing source of challenge and learning. We believe that physical settings—in the organization, at home, and in recreational and other areas—can be important continuing contributors to the users' development or stagnation.

For example, locational factors play a part in peoples' development. A person whose work space is back in a corner, where contact occurs with very few people, will tend not to be stimulated to think of himself and the world in new ways. Similarly, a person located where she comes in contact only with people who think the same way she does (such as may happen in an exclusive housing development or in a homogeneous ghetto area) will not tend to alter her view of the world very much, even though the world and its problems are continuously changing.

Another major factor is the degree to which a setting can be manipulated or altered to suit changing functions or moods. Growth tends to occur when people identify something they would like to do or understand, take action, and get feedback about the results of their actions. Because of its concreteness and visibility, the physical setting is a particularly good medium for engaging in this growth cycle. Settings can be better or worse for stimulating action and learning, however. The more fixed and unalterable the setting, the less useful it is as a stimulator of growth. If everything in the place is finished to the last detail, the designer may have learned a great deal, but the users are unlikely to learn very much beyond how to use what has been provided for them.

There are usually three main causes of fixedness in an organization's settings: (1) the actual design and construction of the facilities; (2) the set of rules and policies which limits the extent to which members are allowed to influence and solve problems about their own settings; and (3) the members' own blindness to their acceptance of settings as "givens" that cannot be altered. The more they treat variable features as fixed, the less potential there is for growth.

Group Growth

Settings can also stimulate growth in entities larger than one individual. Office layouts that encourage free interaction and visibility are often a stimulus to the growth of cohesion and interpersonal competence of a group. Similarly, some of the most interesting team-building sessions we have encountered have been work parties, where a group was "fixing-up" their physical environment to be more suitable for their purposes. In the process of deciding what their goals are, what changes are needed, planning how these changes will be carried out, and actually doing the work, members discover much about one another, about themselves, and about the skills necessary for joint activities.

SUMMARY

To summarize very briefly, the physical setting of an organization can be looked at as both an indicator and cause of climate. Cues about the "feel" of the social climate can be gathered by looking at the location of the system, the external structure, and the shape and quality of the internal spaces of the organization. On the causal side, settings operate as influences on climate through the activities they allow or inhibit, through the symbolic messages they contain, and through the memories and feelings they stimulate in users.

In examining these influences, we discussed examples from each of the four climate dimensions. The discussion was by no means meant to be the last word on the subject and interested readers can find a fuller discussion of settings and organizational life in Steele's recent book.[7]

One final point should be reemphasized. The impact of a particular physical setting on climate is almost never a pure one. Rather, the impact of a setting tends to be a combination of physical factors, the styles of the people attracted by that setting, and the social norms and rules that affect how the physical features are perceived and used. In order to change a setting, we may have to change the facilities, the rules about their use, or (most often) both of these, in order to make a real difference.

NOTES

1.   From John R. Coleman, *Blue Collar Journal: A College President's Sabbatical* (Philadelphia and New York: Lippincott, 1974), p. 208. Copyright © 1974 by John R. Coleman. Reprinted by permission of J.B. Lippincott Company.

2.   C. Northcote Parkinson, "Plans and Plants, or the Administration Block," in *Parkinson's Law and Other Studies in Administration* (Harmondsworth, Middlesex: Penguin, 1959).

3.   For example, see Peter Manning, *Office Design: A Study of Environment* (Liverpool, U.K.: The Pilkington Research Unit, 1965). This study found that employees tended to vandalize their new building much less than the old one.

4. H. Coffey, A. Athos, and P. Reynolds, *Behavior in Organizations: A Multi-Dimensional View* (Englewood Cliffs, N.J.: Prentice-Hall, 1975).

5. Robert Propst, *The Office—A Facility Based on Change* (Zeeland, Michigan: Herman Miller, Inc., 1968).

6. For a full discussion of the effects of greater self-control over one's settings, see Fritz Steele, "Humanizing the Physical Setting at Work," in F. Meltzer and F. Wickert, *Humanizing Organizational Behavior* (Springfield, Illinois: Charles C. Thomas, 1976).

7. Fritz Steele, *Physical Settings and Organizational Development* (Reading, Mass.: Addison-Wesley, 1973).

Chapter 9

Shaping Up the Physical Setting

In this chapter we describe some of the issues and methods related to altering the organization's physical settings as a means of improving the social climate. As elsewhere in the book, we focus on one specific aspect of organizational life and on the way that aspect can be altered to change the system's climate.

It bears repeating, that we do not see organizational dynamics as being such separate processes as this focus implies. The topics are discussed separately for simplicity's sake, but the actual influences are much more circular. While settings do influence organization climate, climate influences what people can do together, which in turn influences decisions that shape their settings. Be that as it may, we want to focus on influencing factors related to the physical setting, as a means of discovering how one can influence the climate. The discussion is in four parts:

- General change targets
- Stimulating change on the four climate dimensions
- Factors that block settings' change
- Illustrative change methods.

GENERAL CHANGE TARGETS

Many different approaches and goals are possible when attempting to improve an organization's physical settings. One useful approach for setting change goals in this area is to be as explicit as you can about the change target: What processes, things, or behaviors are to be altered? To simplify the planning process, we use six categories of change targets.

The level of available knowledge or data about the impact of settings on climate. One way that people are encouraged to do something differently is when they know more about the costs and gains of their present mode and of alternative modes. It helps to make data as available as possible and to try out new forms experimentally, so that people can see the consequences for themselves.

The level of environmental competence of the members of the system. One way of improving settings is to increase the skills of members to shape their settings, to use them well, and to diagnose problems so that they can change when appropriate.

The physical facilities themselves. If one plans to improve settings, changing them physically is the action usually contemplated. As we will discuss below, this is an important target; but, as you can see from this list, it is only one of a number of targets which can be changed.

The patterns of use of facilities. The impact of facilities is controlled considerably by *how* people use them: the patterns that develop about what is and is not done in various rooms and spaces; the uses to which work spaces can be put; the relative placement of people within a work area; and so on. The climate can be changed by altering use patterns and thereby changing people's experiences.

Decision processes about facilities. A key factor in people's experiencing of their environment is their perception of how much they can influence their own life space. The climate in an organization can therefore be changed by making changes in the way facilities decisions are made. The opportunities for change are primarily in the direction of a looser, more personally oriented climate, since the present pattern in most United States work organizations is for physical-setting decisions to be heavily controlled by the top levels in the system.[1]

Choices about where to do different activities. The impact of your setting is also partly determined by *where* you choose to do things. Many people fight uphill battles against their surroundings because they have made a bad choice about location for an activity. We will not deal directly with this problem here, but interested readers should see a recent piece called "The Scene of the Crime,"[2] which deals with locational choices in the consulting process.

STIMULATING THE CLIMATE DIMENSIONS

The target areas listed above are a way of conceptualizing the commodities you are trying to change. From the standpoint of the *effects* you are trying to achieve with this change, we find it useful to use the four climate dimensions. In this section we will provide some examples of the kinds of changes that could be made in settings or settings management in order to stimulate improvement on each dimension. Since the impact of actions does not necessarily fall in exclusive categories, we have listed examples under their primary dimension and indicated in parentheses and italics when they are likely to affect other dimensions also.

The Amount of Human Energy in the System

Enhancing Visual Stimulation. A lot of work has been done in this area over the last few years. Primary colors (versus institutional greens and greys) can provide a more visually exciting environment, as do graphic designs (such as so-called "supergraphics") that stimulate new reaction patterns. The emphasis here would be on stimulation, surprise, and excitement as opposed to steady, traditional, regular patterns oriented toward stability and security.

Spaces for Human Contacts. Another way of enhancing system energy is to increase the probability that *people* (not things) will stimulate one another to consider or take new actions, set new goals, or whatever. This probability can be raised by increasing the number of usable settings where contact can take place. New meeting rooms (which are often very limited), lounge areas, and central gathering spaces can increase mutual contact.

For example, one new high school was built around an open central courtyard which was a perfect gathering place for students. It was *so* good, in fact, that the school administration made a rule that students could not "loiter" there, since the administrators felt that the energy generated would be used toward rebellious ends.

Altering the Amount of Space to Fit Task Needs.   The energy costs of being too cramped are well known, especially in growing organizations. Less obvious is the depressing, energy-draining effect that *too much* space can have on a firm that is in a period of contraction. One executive told us that the emptiness kept reminding him of former good times and it didn't seem to him like a "critical mass" of activity was going on. Organizations in this stage would gain more than just a short-term cost savings by shifting to a smaller, different setting without visual cues to trigger memories of past heydays.

Distribution of Energy

These examples are aimed at improving the uses to which energy is put in the system.

Reshaping Boundary Areas.   Unproductive rivalries and conflicts between groups that should be collaborating are often encouraged or maintained by little or no contact between members of the two groups. One of the ways of increasing contact is to reduce physical barriers: move the groups closer together, reduce obstacles that restrict movement at the boundary, and create symbolic messages (such as the welcome mat) that encourage flow between the groups rather than discourage it. (*This can also enhance the pleasure that people get from working there.*)

A client firm recently reduced the insularity of its marketing group by designing another door opening into the market group's spaces. Until then, there had only been one (rather torturous) route by which Production and Engineering people could "stop by" and talk to anyone in marketing.

Reducing Distances between People.   This is an obvious means of reducing the amount of time and energy spent in travel

"I don't think the Creative Department and Account Services have been really 'listening for understanding' with each other."

or related linking activities. The distance to be reduced can be linear (the amount) or functional (the degree of hassle that it takes to get from one point to another, such as having to use the elevator each time you go to someone's office).

Reducing the Status Emphasis on Physical-Setting Features. In most organizations, physical features serve double duty as task facilitators and as symbolic language indicators that people use to place themselves and one another in the hierarchy. These two functions often conflict with each other, so that a good task arrangement may not send the right status messages. The status function tends to get the nod, with a resulting cost of energy going into calculating the pecking order rather than into productive efforts. One company has countered this drain by assigning the different hierarchical levels code numbers that are displayed on desk plaques; facilities are distributed, shifted, changed, returned to central supply, etc., based on who needs them for their tasks rather than on status level.

Changing Norms and Policies about Use of Settings. As we mentioned above, norms and policies can control how effectively the settings fit users' needs. Changes have been made in several organizations to place decision making about use of facilities in the hands of the users, in order to save energy that used to go into (a) justifications to higher management and (b) inventing and implementing ways to get around the most constraining and inefficient rules.[3]

Building In More Flexibility when Creating New Settings or Altering Old Ones. If the setting is designed to be changed with little major technical alteration, then it is more likely to be appropriate for the range of activities that people engage in and for needs that change over time. Examples would be Robert Propst's "Action Office II," a set of components which can be organized and reorganized by the user in a number of different ways[4]; movable walls and partition systems; and electrical/mechanical grid systems that do not require fixed locations for work stations. (*These inputs can also increase the sense of pleasure people get from being in their work spaces.*)

Pleasure

Support for Personalization. This is probably the most important step toward helping people enjoy their settings more. If employees can influence their immediate work areas in ways that reflect themselves, then top management does not have to come up with grand schemes that delight everyone (which is generally impossible, anyway). What *is* required is (a) not to have numerous rules that make it impossible for people to do anything personal to their place; (b) to design flexible work settings that are not so finished nor so spartan that a person can't include items that reflect family, hobbies, or values; and (c) possibly to provide a selection of facilities to choose from (desks, chairs, fabrics, colors, etc.), so that a manageable number of choices leads to real individualization of work areas.

More Attention to "No-Person's Lands." Work organizations have many areas that no one feels free to influence. These are the no-person's lands that are not the work space of any particular person or group, such as corridors, supply rooms, some reception zones, and the like. As a result, these tend to be visually and tactilely dead areas, usually the least stimulating in the building. And yet people experience these dead settings all day long; many spend more time in them than in any private space of their own.

Effort should be put into bringing these areas alive. TV stations and advertising agencies sometimes use their corridors as display areas for shows, clients' products, etc. M.I.T. placed removable contact paper on the walls of their very long (and heavily used) main corridor and encouraged students to decorate it any way they liked. The results were notable, both in terms of enjoyment of the process of creation and for the visual excitement that movement through the corridor now provides.

The argument is often used that no one should decorate no-person's lands because one person's choices might not be good for other people passing through; but we believe that somebody's positive action is better than stretches of wasteland all over the system.

Another possibility is to *play* more with dead spaces, such as doing graphics and hanging sculptures for interior light wells — those notorious visually dead spaces that proliferated in office buildings of the thirties and forties.

New Facilities May Be Better — But Not Necessarily. If facilities are so bad that people can't control basic distractions like rodents, cold, water, noise crowding, etc., then creating new facilities can enhance the climate and the users' enjoyment of the setting. But many firms have had the experience of building a brand-new setting, moving in, and finding that they enjoy it less than the old. The climate is worse, when it should have gotten better.

What happened? A number of factors are usually operating: the new facilities are often cold, slick, and so "functionally designed" that they have no connection with the human beings who must use them; the old facilities were quite influenceable — in fact, they had to be influenced in order to be usable — whereas the new setting is totally finished before the people ever get there. In addition, new rules are usually created to keep users from "damaging" the new facilities.

Our suggestions are: (a) organizations should think carefully before building a totally new facility — rehabilitation of the old one may be less costly in terms of money *and* human enjoyment; and (b) if new facilities are built, the decision processes and subsequent management of the facilities should be carefully controlled so that the users don't become overcontrolled.

Growth

Maintaining a Demanding Environment. A setting that demands that something be done with it in order for it to be used is more likely to promote growth than one totally finished by nonusers. People are required to think about their goals, the activities they will use to reach them, and the physical features that should support these activities. This kind of practice improves problem-solving skills for both individuals and groups and lessens their dependence on higher management for resources and conflict resolution.

Sharing Decision Making with Users.   The above point is related to allowing people to influence their settings, as well as requiring that they do so. Decision processes that include the ultimate user are likely to promote growth in the users' abilities, as do task decisions that allow people to test themselves and receive feedback about the consequences of their actions.

Technical Support for Tinkering (Building In Changeability and Manipulability).   If facilities are designed with flexible technologies, they encourage people to explore their possibilities. As a very simple example, movable furniture invites and supports a variety of uses, unlike fixed furniture that must stay in one particular arrangement. A key feature of a growth-producing climate is that people's activities and styles can vary over time, as needs, moods, and interests change, *without* requiring major inputs of time, money, and equipment in order to make physical-system changes.

These, then, are some examples of how you would think about the problem of using the physical setting (and the social processes that control it) to stimulate improvement on the four climate dimensions. These examples are summarized in Table 9.1.

FACTORS THAT BLOCK THE CHANGE PROCESS

When you try to influence anything in an organization, you are usually dealing with a whole network of interrelated processes that tend to support or block each other. Physical settings and their management are no exception to this rule. Attempts to change climate in this area are likely to run counter to several key forces that exist in most work organizations. We will describe these forces briefly, not because there are simple answers to how to overcome them, but because being aware of them can help you to make sense out of what looks like a random pattern of reactions and resistances to your efforts. Following a description of three main factors, we will provide a sample of some of the methods we have used to effect changes in settings.

Table 9.1
Actions Involving Physical Setting which Stimulate Change in Organization Climate

Stimulating Energy	Climate Dimension		
	Improving the Distribution of Energy	*Increasing Pleasure*	*Improving Growth Possibilities*
Visual stimulation - colors, graphics, etc.	Reducing boundary barriers between groups	Support for personalization	Creating demand quality in settings
Central gathering places	Reducing actual and functional distances	Livening up dead zones — no-person's lands, light wells, etc.	Sharing decision processes with users
More meeting places	Reducing emphasis on the status function of facilities	Avoiding sterility of slick new facilities	Technical support for tinkering
Changing the size of spaces	Building-in flexibility (physical and social)		

Proprietary Thinking

Within the pattern of an organization's power differences and balances, top executives generally think it is their duty (and their right) to be proprietary about the system's physical facilities. They dole out goodies as if they were door prizes, usually basing their decisions on the degree to which receivers fit company norms about "rewardable" people. The doling-out function tends to be most jealously protected in those organizations where people do not find their work tasks to be very intrinsically rewarding. This pattern also fits the top-down control mode of treating subordinates as not competent to manage their settings.

Fantasies of Perfection

As in other areas of organizational problem solving, managers who control facilities tend to believe there is only one aesthetically "right" solution to each physical-settings problem. They therefore tend to think that their mission is to discover that perfect solution and make it happen. The implementation may be through imposing it unilaterally or through "selling it" to the users ("once they understand it, they'll accept it"). In either mode, the underlying belief is that there is only one right way, rather than the alternative assumption (which we believe) that there are usually a number of acceptable alternatives to most design problems. Which is the "best" choice depends on who the users are, what the particular time period calls for, and how the decision itself is made.

Focus on Conspicuous Costs

Perhaps one of the biggest problems we face in this area is getting managers to recognize that there are more organizational problems in the physical setting's impact than meet the eye. When decisions about facilities are being considered, people tend to focus on certain criteria to the exclusion of others. Traditionally, organizations have paid most attention to selected money costs, such as initial installation and maintenance costs of the new facilities. They have paid much less attention to the less-quantifiable costs to the human organization (low energy, blocked growth, decreased vitality, decreased mutual stimulation, etc.) of physically shaping the system in economical but inadequate ways.

The capital outlays are the conspicuous costs, so they are weighted heavily. The human system costs and gains are inconspicuous, hard to quantify, and may depend in part on how the change process is handled. Consequently, they usually are pushed aside during the decision process, given the general preference for certainty over ambiguity. The inconspicuous costs are likely to become visible only over time. When people are moved from a setting that they could influence considerably into an antiseptic setting over which they have no control, they often express their displeasure through such means as increased sick leave, lateness, and general inefficiency in the new location. It is our hope that this book will help readers to make better cases for the very real human costs of bad settings and oppressive organization climate.

SOME CHANGE METHODS

If you want to improve your climate by changing the physical setting in ways discussed earlier (or in others, for that matter) and you are up against the counterforces just outlined, what can be done? A sampling of some specific methods used to stimulate changes in the design and/or use of settings follows. After each heading we note (in parentheses) which general change areas, as described at the beginning of this chapter, are the primary targets of that method.

Space Awareness Workshops (Environmental Competence)

Various programs have been designed specifically to increase clients' environmental competence skills, with a particular focus on expanding their awareness of the impact of their various settings. We have conducted these workshops both at conference centers and in the system's spaces. The obvious advantage to doing it in the system is that specific real examples can be used and it is therefore easier to generalize about how to apply principles to the present settings.

These programs emphasize experiential training exercises that ask people to examine their own responses to various elements and patterns in the setting. Although we will not reproduce specific exercises here, interested readers can find useful examples in Steele's book on physical organization development[5] or the early volume on Gestalt therapy by Perls et al.[6]

Our experience with these workshops has shown that people often start with a fairly low level of spatial awareness, so that a one-day or one-and-a-half-day workshop can dramatically open peoples' eyes to the variety of ways they are influenced by their work places, homes, and other settings. They quickly appreciate the fact that some of the weather or "feel" of their work place is directly related to choices about facilities.

Teaching a Diagnostic System (Environmental Competence; Data Generation)

This process is aimed at equipping people to make a specific analysis of the adequacy of their work setting using a six-dimensional functional-analysis system developed by Steele.[7] The six dimensions or functions of settings are:

a. Shelter and Security
b. Social Contact
c. Symbolic Identification
d. Task Instrumentality
e. Pleasure
f. Growth

The Pleasure and Growth functions relate directly to the similarly named climate dimensions, while a–d contribute in various ways to the amount of energy in the system and how effectively it is distributed for productive ends. (A number of examples have already been considered in the section, "Stimulating the Climate Dimensions," earlier in this chapter.)

We teach the concepts of the six functions and help people practice using them analytically. This provides them with a concrete tool and reduces the mystery that sometimes surrounds how we (as consultants) have been arriving at inferences about the organization's climate based on physical clues. The clients soon realize that what we were seeing was there for all to see.

Use-Pattern Analysis (Generation of Shared Data; Analyzing Use Patterns)

In addition to considering the impact of features of the setting, it is also useful to help people examine the other half of the interaction: the ways in which the setting's impact on climate is controlled by their own policies, norms, and habits governing ways to use the facilities. This usually involves a two- to three-hour session devoted to describing as many of these influences as possible; then exploring their consequences in terms of what the place feels like to the users; and finally making some choices about which patterns should be kept and what new ones should be formally or informally instituted.

In one group where this analysis was carried out, members made (what turned out to be) a key decision to drop the rule that no one could bring to their work space any furniture or decorations of their own from outside the company. The feared competitive status race did not materialize, but increased feelings of fun in being at work certainly did. ("It finally feels like I'm at home here," one person said later.)

Designer Consultation (Facilities Change)

Professional designers are beginning to take more of an interest in the behavioral aspects of their work. When an organization wishes to liven up its settings, it can obtain both creative ideas and technical guidance by consulting a designer who has interests in group and organizational dynamics. Other designers might just as well provide the ideas and guidance, but the climate often stays the same or gets worse, since they are not sensitive to how their own processes (such as trying to demand control over how members use the newly designed setting) can contribute to the very problems that were draining energy or pleasure to begin with. Designers who are aware of the impact of their own influence processes tend to be able to work collaboratively rather than autocratically with a client system.

Demonstration Rides (Facilities Change; Decision Processes; Data Generation)

In many instances, people who are asked to consider new alternatives in shaping their settings tend to be wary or suspicious of new elements they have never experienced. Rather than ordering them to cooperate or trying to wear them down with arguments, we have recommended that management try the "Demonstration Ride" (DR).

The DR is simply an experimental process where a new alternative is tried by a particular subgroup (not the whole system) that is interested and willing to try it out. For example, we recently had a case in which one group chose to do an open landscape plan—something that top management was selling but many subordinates weren't buying. It was relatively simple to define this group's area as an experimental zone and then to make changes and see how it went. Their experiences were positive, others could see the benefits for themselves, and the other groups were convinced to switch to an open plan.

Of course, the DR cannot be used for large-scale, irreversible decisions such as the geographic location of the whole system, but in a surprising number of change areas action does not have to be taken all at once. Rather, it can be carried out as a sequential data-generating process with actual built-in experiences.

THREE GENERAL PRINCIPLES

In closing this chapter, we will summarize three principles or generalizations that lie behind many of the suggestions offered for changing settings.

The Principle of Minimal Constraints

In order to have the physical setting contribute to an alive, vital organization climate in your system, you should work on a principle of minimal constraints, so that people feel free to shape desired environments for themselves (something that is very hard to do with the physical weather, except by moving).

As we have already discussed, a policy of minimal constraints would include: (a) built-in flexibility so that settings can
be used in a variety of ways without high money or energy costs
for each change of shape; (b) rules about use which are kept to
the necessary minimum and are designed, as much as possible,
to facilitate rather than limit actual use of the facilities; and (c)
support and training in environmental competence for the users,
so that they have at least as good a chance to use the setting well
as they would have in other endeavors management wanted to
encourage.

We feel that the minimal-constraints principle is worth repeating here, because most organizations seem to work on a
maximal-constraints principle. They build inflexible, rigid facilities; they develop fixed, "fail-safe" rules and policies to cover all
possible contingencies in advance (rather than dealing with some
isolated cases as they arise); and they provide no training in environmental competence and yet are surprised (and self-
righteous) when subordinates don't use new facilities well.

A Person's Relationship to the Work Setting Is a Process, Not a One-Shot Event

According to this principle, it is very important that managers concern themselves not only with the design of new facilities, but also with the design of new feedback processes that will
help members' experiences become data for reshaping the
setting as times and needs change. The setting should be a live
contributor to the climate—not a dead, static monument to past
needs or fantasies. This need for a feedback process is very similar to the need for self-correcting social processes, as discussed
in Chapter 5.

The Physical and Social Aspects of an Organization Are Part of an Interlocking System

People tend to meet their needs through a combination of
social and physical solutions. For example, one can gain some
needed privacy by shutting one's door (physical) or by signalling
that people should leave one alone, thereby drawing on a norm
about when people should not talk to others (social). Change

efforts in the physical settings should be done with this view-point in mind. If you change the physical setting, you are likely to have to readjust some social norms as well; and, if you want to change the social setting, it often is helpful (or even essential) to change the physical setting to support this change.

NOTES

1. See F. Steele, "The Top-Down Society: Spatial Decisions in the Organizational World," *Environment/Planning and Design* (Summer 1971): 24-30.

2. In Fritz Steele, *Consulting for Organizational Change* (Amherst, Mass.: University of Massachusetts Press, 1975).

3. The possibilities for change in rules about use are strongly limited when top management has a strong investment in using these rules to demonstrate that it has the power and no one else does. In these cases, the issue is clearly not a rational one of what would create the best climate.

4. See Robert Propst, *The Office—A Facility Based on Change* (Zeeland, Mich.: Herman Miller, 1968).

5. Fritz Steele, *Physical Settings and Organization Development* (Reading, Mass.: Addison-Wesley, 1973), Chapter 12.

6. F. Perls, R. Hefferline, and P. Goodman, *Gestalt Therapy* (New York: Julian Press (also a Delta Paperback), 1951). See the section called "Contacting the Environment."

7. Fritz Steele, *Physical Settings and Organization Development* (Reading, Mass.: Addison-Wesley, 1973), Chapters 4-10.

Chapter 10

Communication and Climate

Communication, as influenced by the level of *disclosure* that people practice with one another, can significantly affect an organization's climate. By disclosure we mean the process often associated with "openness": sharing information (ideas or feelings) with other members of the system. Although we limit our discussion to internal disclosure (within the system), one could also look at external disclosure—how much the organization exposes to the outside world.

Emphasis here is on *patterns* of disclosure rather than on low disclosure or high disclosure at a particular moment or by a particular person. Everyone makes choices about what to share and what not to share with other people; not to do so would be to overwhelm both others and oneself with a continuous flow of ideas, images, and stimuli. Our interest, therefore, is not in disclosure *per se*, but rather in the patterns of disclosure within groups and organizations and the effects these disclosure patterns have on the climate. A disclosure pattern is described by the average level of disclosure in the system: the pattern of who discloses and who doesn't, who is disclosed to and who is not, the topics that can be openly discussed, and the legitimate settings where people can disclose. Some organizations have clear patterns in these areas; some are less consistent, and vary from time to time or within different groups in the system.

THE NATURE OF DISCLOSURE

In order to explore the impact of different disclosure patterns on organization climate, we need to describe briefly the process of disclosure as we define it. Disclosure simply means sharing or showing to another person something that is true about oneself. That can be a feeling, an opinion, an accomplishment, something one would like to do, information that one has but the other person does not, and so on. Sidney Jourard used disclosure to mean one specific part of this collection—namely, an individual revealing to others those internal feelings, aspirations, opinions, and values that are central to his or her definition of self.[1] We are looking at disclosure in a broader sense than Jourard, since we are specifically interested in disclosure as a phenomenon in organizations, where many different kinds of information sharing are possible—some related to self, some to social relationships, and some to the tasks being performed. It is important also to note that inside the organization disclosure can take place between individuals and between groups. Both of these are included in our use of disclosure: a sharing with another person or group of relevant information that you have but they do not.

This definition is related to but not synonymous with what management theorists and organization members mean when they talk about the need for good communication in an organization. The communication process has most often been discussed as if it were basically a technical problem, solved by better techniques and channels for transmitting information. In this discussion, we see disclosure as communication to others, but also as much more than a technical process. It is part of the process of self-definition of individuals and groups; it is part of the process of reality testing and creation of a shared world view; it is a determinant of the very language by which people communicate in a specific organization; and it is both a cause and a reflection of the climate of the system—the atmosphere that surrounds members in their day-to-day work space.

Disclosure behavior in an organization is related to Carl Rogers' concept called "The Facts are Friendly,"[2] based on the assumption that if something is true, then it is generally more useful to have it visible and accurately represented than to have it hidden or distorted. This holds for ideas and opinions as well as for feelings about oneself, others, or events.

The long-term energy costs of a system operating as if the facts were *not* friendly is graphically illustrated by Solzhenitsyn's description of the tribulations of Soviet academic efforts during the Stalin era:

"Weeding out the foreigners" meant going through the thesis throwing out every reference to a foreigner: "As Lowe has shown," for instance, would have to read, "As scientists have shown"; "As Langmuir has demonstrated" would become "As has been demonstrated." On the other hand, if a Russian, or a Russified Dane or German had done anything at all to distinguish himself, then you had to give his full name and duly bring out his great patriotism and immortal services to science.[3]

It literally required man-years of effort to describe the facts of science as they *should* have happened, not as they actually did.

Argyris has called straightforward disclosure the "owning" of one's ideas and feelings, which means bringing out into the open (where it can be seen by others) what one thinks and feels about what is going on. The more a person believes that the facts are friendly and that one should publicly "own" his or her thoughts and feelings, the more that person will tend to disclose. There are two crucial aspects to this relatively simple statement: one is for the person to *recognize* that he or she has information to disclose; the other is to care that the information might be *useful* to another person.

Recognition

In the work culture of our society, people are actually trained to be blind to information they have which could be useful if disclosed. In many systems, feelings are considered to be irrelevant and not task oriented, and are therefore not shared, even when the disclosure of a feeling could help clarify what is happening. For example, people will find clever ways of resisting the "railroading" of a decision by a boss or committee chairman without ever letting that person know that it is the process of railroading which they resent, not the specific decision (which they may actually support!).

The choice not to disclose angry feelings is very often not a conscious one based on weighing advantages and disadvantages. Instead, people, if they are like those in most work organizations, do not even *recognize* the feelings as information available for disclosure (and being held back). After all, isn't it more "mature" to "keep personalities out of things"? Most organization leaders expect their members to be blind to a number of (potentially useful) areas. Feelings tend to be a common blind spot, but there are others: perceptions of processes of interaction; disagreements with those who have power over one; possibilities for different perceptions of the same event; motives for differing goals among members of the same group, and so on.

Usefulness

When people behave in a high-disclosure manner, they tend to define "relevance" broadly and are willing to share information if there is some *possibility* that it can be useful or helpful to someone (or help themselves by sharing). By contrast, a low-disclosure situation has inherent in it a very narrow definition of relevance, often with the apparent goal of being *sure* that information is useful before it is shared. A low-disclosing person usually adheres to a strict (internal) test of relevance for a particular disclosure and makes this test unilaterally (because shared testing of relevance would involve disclosure).

For a simple example, consider the following from an interview after a staff meeting:

Interviewer:	Were there particular things which you thought about but decided not to mention during the meeting?
Mr. A:	Oh sure, several of them: (*lists them*).
Interviewer:	Well, for example, why didn't you bring up the staffing problem with John?
Mr. A:	I had to make a judgment there, and I decided that it wasn't relevant to what we were doing or to his problem.[4]

This type of unilateral testing is presumably intended to maximize the usefulness of a single piece of information to the receiver. It often has the additional *unintended* effect of reducing the probability of needed information being available at the right time, because the test is made by the *sender* unilaterally. He or she is usually not in as good a position to judge usefulness to the receiver as is the receiver.

In an organizational context, this unilateral test for relevance is formalized into what is often called "the need to know" policy, where those in higher power positions disclose to those in lower positions what they (the highers) decide that they (the lowers) really need to know in order to do their (the lowers') jobs. If someone has information to disclose which he knows would be useful but fears that he would be punished for disclosing it, because it does not meet some (real or imagined) test of relevance, he is likely to withhold the disclosure, especially if it involves tentative thoughts and feelings. In this kind of system, over time, people lose their ability accurately to perceive and be aware of their own opinions and feelings. Their energy is directed at suppression rather than exploration.

SOME DIMENSIONS OF DISCLOSURE

The quality of an organization's disclosure pattern can be explored on many different dimensions. For illustration, we will touch on three of the most important: the private/public split, the range of acceptable topics, and the normative system.

The Private/Public Split

One factor that influences disclosure climates is the private/public distinction. People tend to define their settings as either "public" or "private" and have different rules about disclosure in each setting. For instance, a small group of people can talk about common problems freely over lunch (private) where they say many things they would never disclose in a formal staff meeting (public), even though the meeting may consist primarily of the same people! Also, a meeting between a boss and his or her subordinate in the boss's office is private, but the same conversation in the boss's staff meeting is public, particularly for such topic areas as their views of one another's performance or potential. In this example, the other members of the staff get defined as "the public" and the familiar rule, "you shouldn't wash your dirty linen in public," gets applied.

The reason we have found this distinction to be an important one is fairly obvious: *the definition of public and private settings is to some extent an arbitrary one*, and is made differently by different groups and organizations. Moreover, the definitions that settings receive determine what kind of disclosure goes on, and therefore what it feels like to work there. For example, a marketing group that defines itself as private and joint meetings of the group and manufacturing people as public will tend to disclose less to the manufacturing people. They may send out what we call "press releases": carefully worded pictures of market forecasts, manpower, etc. that vary from their actual information and are designed to create the right public image of their group. If the manufacturing people then make their decisions, such as production schedules, based on the press releases, they may unknowingly put excessive demands on the marketing group —demands that would not be excessive if the press releases were true. The marketing group will use the (perceived) excessive demands as confirmation of the fact that manufacturing does not have marketing's interest at heart. Manufacturing gets defined even more as "them," or "the public," and receives even more careful press releases in the future.

Thus, low disclosure can often trigger a cycle of increasing misperceptions. In the reverse direction, high disclosure can often break that cycle and promote high disclosure in the other person, which supports further disclosure in the first person, and so on. Which direction this process tends to go will often depend on the public/private distinctions. The higher the need for shared information between individuals and groups, the higher the costs when most settings are defined as public and the greater the gains if they can be seen as private.

Allowable Topic Range

A second dimension of disclosure is the range of topics that are shared. In a high-disclosure system, there are relatively few rules about what can and cannot be discussed. People talk about ideas, opinions, agreement with others, disagreements, feelings, themselves, reactions to others, processes that are going on inside the system, outside trends, areas where improvement is needed, new alternatives, likes and dislikes, and so on. Whatever is true and descriptive of themselves and their world can be shared and examined, without a great deal of thought and planning beforehand as to whether a particular statement will or will not be acceptable. Obviously, this pattern of disclosure is closely associated with what we call an atmosphere of spontaneity, and often with an air of vitality as well. The topic range open for "public" discussion is very broad and there are few sanctions for the act of disclosure itself.

The gains from this free-ranging discussion mode have even been touted by one analyst for that most redoubtable of bureaucracies, the British Civil Service:

> It might be better, too, if the major policy issues were discussed by a departmental board, again of fairly wide membership, before formal advice was tendered to ministers. This would ensure that the advice had at least been tried in a circle of people who were not only generally knowledgeable about the background of the questions but about the people tendering the advice. The measure of internal openness which such a system would give would be at least some safeguard to a Minister and ensure that he was receiving something like the best Departmental advice and not merely the flattery of a courtier whose chief skill was in scenting what his master wanted to hear, and speaking accordingly. Combined with a system of canvassing views about possible promotions, it could in time exercise a considerable influence on the efficiency of the system.[5]

As this passage also implies, at the other end of the scale from a system where spontaneity is the norm is the system where a great deal of calculation is used to decide what gets shared and what does not. Specific topic areas are ruled out of bounds as far as open discussions are concerned, and those who are successful in the system know which areas are "taboo" (i.e., unspeakable) and how to deal with them (when absolutely necessary) without actually talking about them.

Our research indicates that a number of topics crop up quite frequently on organizations' lists of informal taboos. Some of these are:

- Feelings, emotions, and other areas labelled as non-"facts"
- Pay, salary, and the reward system in general
- Likes and dislikes of people, and reasons for them
- Evaluations of performance (in public)
- Promotions, career plans, placement decisions (not to be raised by the person in front of those who control his or her career)

- Disagreements between hierarchical levels (when others are present)
- Disagreements or conflicts that might be embarrassing to the discloser or the receiver (or some third party).

There are, of course, many other taboos in specific organizations and not all of these occur in every system, but these seem to be generally regarded as areas where disclosure and open discussion are inappropriate and even dangerous.

The major cost of taboos in systems is not the embarrassing fact of their existence, but rather the untouchable areas they create. When a topic, such as career difficulties, is taboo, it is unlikely that members of a group will be able to even see the size of the problem, let alone share enough information to discover the best alternative solutions. Taboos therefore create problem areas in which the members are guaranteed to be incompetent.

The Normative System

The third factor influencing disclosure patterns is the normative system which supports or inhibits disclosure. In Chapter 4 we discussed how norms help create energy, affect distribution, contribute to pleasure, and promote growth. They also have a major effect on the relative amount of disclosure and the topic areas discussed. Norms that promote disclosure place a positive value on openness, testing topic relevance with others, and in general talking about feelings as well as topics. Norms that inhibit disclosure identify many subjects as private and serve to perpetuate the organization's list of taboos.

One particularly important norm against disclosure in many organizations is the previously mentioned "supernorm" against talking about norms. In effect, it is often taboo to talk about the taboos. Of course, norms that required the disclosure of everything would also be destructive, because people (and systems) can become very bogged down with "data overload." The question is one of balance, or how to develop norms that support an appropriate level of disclosure in an organization.

Our image of a vital, alive, organization is one where there is support for open disclosure, a commitment to work through major issues as they arise, and a competence to sort out which issues should be worked through, so that not everything raised must be laboriously followed up. As we noted earlier, it is the sense of incompetence at choosing among possible issues which often acts as a major block to raising issues or sharing perceptions in the first place.

DISCLOSURE AND THE WEATHER

High and low disclosure can have a decisive impact on the climate of an organization or group. In the following discussion we use our earlier criteria of climate effects: total energy, distribution of energy, pleasure, and growth.

Total Energy Available

One impact of a low-disclosure climate is to reduce risk taking. People have learned that when in doubt about whether to say something because it might (or will) violate a rule, it is wiser in terms of career survival to say or do nothing at all. Low-disclosure climates often legitimize the choice of total inaction when a risk exists, and thus reduce the amount of organizational energy available for action.

A second drain on energy from a low-disclosure climate is more subtle. Research on small-group task performance under different communication patterns has found that low disclosure blocks the mobilization of a system's energy by inhibiting its members' ability to organize themselves for tasks, thus essentially neutralizing potential energy that has no outlet channels[6]. If alternative structures are undiscussable or unrecognized, the group tends to stay locked in its first structure.

By contrast, the high-disclosure climate is characterized by spontaneity, where the sharing of ideas and feelings is valued and appreciated both as a task contribution and as an exercise that keeps the system vital for the times when very specific information will be critically needed. It is not necessary to dissipate much energy calculating whether to say things that you think are important to share, as long as you are able to discriminate between which items need more attention and which do not.

It may be, however, that some types of low-disclosure climates can contribute to keeping the energy in a system at a higher level than it would otherwise be. For example, leaders of large systems (such as the United States president) often withhold information about their own doubts, fears, or about the magnitude of a threat, because of the possibility that the members of the system would be so discouraged that they would lose all motivation and give up. Similarly, groups in competition often maintain a high esprit de corps and high activity level at their task by screening out positive information about their competitor groups and highlighting the negative information.

Another way in which high disclosure can sap vitality and energy in a system is the phenomenon of "all talk and no action." In some groups the process of disclosure and discussion can be used as a substitute for concrete action. The all-talk, low-action organization has the feel of a hot tropical climate—everything takes a little longer and most people seem a bit groggy or sluggish.

One final aspect of low disclosure and system energy should be mentioned: low disclosure can be a *result* of low system energy as well as a cause. One reason people do not share information openly is that they may be called on to follow up on the information or to work through the reactions that it causes. It takes more energy to deal with an issue on the spot, in the present, than it does to put it off to some vague, undefined time in the future when "it might be more appropriate." Groups that do not have vitality often disclose less because they do not feel they have energy to work on very much. Of course, this stance can also be a rationalization; their energy level may be all right, but they fear the embarrassments that might occur in an open discussion of an issue.

Distribution of Energy

Disclosure patterns affect the use or distribution of organizational energy in many ways. For instance, if promotional and career data are considered taboo and are never talked about openly, people become more nervous about their own standing in the system, even though the rationale for secrecy is usually that "if we don't talk about it, there won't be as much concern about it or as many misleading rumors floating around." The fact is that individuals need to have information about the parts of their world that can substantially influence their futures, and if

"Okay, then, in two weeks we'll begin."

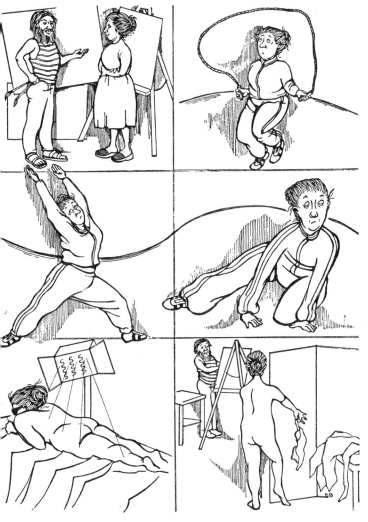

"Sorry, ma'am, I only do faces."

that information is not "officially" available, then time and energy will be channeled into speculating, worrying, and generating rumors that help to fill this information gap. We have seen numerous organizations where the spawning and testing of rumors used up at least as much time as did work on the real tasks of the system. These systems tend to be those with fairly tight rules about what can and can not be talked about directly, particularly between superior and subordinate.

In a related area, employee-evaluation systems that appear to judge members on their image, apparent confidence, smoothness, etc., rather than on what they contribute toward the goals of the system, focus energy on simple survival, particularly if bosses' evaluations are not disclosed directly. The employee is anxious to protect himself or herself against negative images that might be transmitted to those who control one's destiny, particularly if the person regularly receives a type of half-disclosure which we have termed the Unusable Negative Cue. The UNC is a hint from another person (boss, peer, etc.) that you are hurting your image, but the hint is given in a climate that discourages open discussion of the issue — to do so would definitely hurt your image![7]

If an organization systematically excludes certain problems or areas from open disclosure, then much excess energy will be required in order to carry out any task involving these taboo topics. People will have to share information without actually talking about the problem or the issue directly, and this almost always takes longer. We have seen groups go to elaborate lengths, including massive preparations of superfluous data, in order to get an undiscussable message across to a superior or to another group. In addition, the roundabout route is more susceptible to distortion, false starts, wasted motion, and the like than are more direct communications.

In his classic study of managerial behavior, Dalton described this energy drain very clearly:

> Because the internal power struggles of business and industry are largely denied and must be cloaked, it is clear that the ferment of unofficial activities may be more intense than the frankly parliamentary action.... The formal meeting is a gallery of fronts where aimless, devious, and central currents of action merge for a moment, per-

functorily for some, emotionally for others. All depart with new knowledge to pursue variously altered, but rarely the agreed, courses.[8]

We would agree that the costs of a low-disclosure climate are probably nowhere more evident than in the proliferation of unproductive meetings. For instance, the tactful nondisagreement with superiors in a "public" setting can lead to many meetings that are charades; the "united front," or agreement of superior and subordinate, is an established rule recognized by everyone at the meeting, and when the possibility of a difference arises between a boss and a subordinate, everyone there knows that no real questioning or thought can be done until the two of them check it out "in private."

This is a costly definition of public and private, since it leads to extra meetings and to expanded time drains playing out meetings when nothing more can happen. It also adds to the profusion of meetings before the meeting, aimed at making sure that (predictable) disagreements are checked ahead of time. And no new and joint thinking can go on in a session where each person feels bound not to share new ideas that have not been checked out in advance.

Low disclosure between groups is another cause of unproductive uses of organizational energy. The literature is filled with examples of inappropriate intergroup competition between groups that need to collaborate in order for the larger system to function effectively. Subsystems like the marketing and manufacturing areas often spend as much time formulating appropriate press releases for one another as they do working on their tasks. As we said earlier, if the other group acts on the information in the press release, they will probably be acting inappropriately for the needs of the first group, which increases resentment and lowers trust even further.

High disclosure does not always lead to a good distribution of energy, however. If there is very high disclosure in a group, so many issues may be raised that most of the group's energy is spent working on its own internal processes rather than the task. This danger could be met without stifling vitality, however. An effective climate would include a norm that said that people will cut down on disclosure when it *becomes* a problem rather than stopping in advance because it *might get to be* a problem.

Pleasure

How does the pattern of disclosure in a system affect the enjoyment of its members? The issue here is literally how it *feels* to be in climates characterized by high and low disclosure. What is the weather like in these different systems and how much pleasure do they provide to their members?

The first generalization we can make is that, like geographical climate, the effect of different levels of disclosure on people's enjoyment depends to some extent on the people themselves and their individual preferences or moods. For instance, a company president in one organizational study was observed to do all his managing and conflict resolution in one-to-one conferences, and he was very uncomfortable with open disclosure of his own or others in any larger setting. As he described it, he didn't enjoy open discussion; it made him uncomfortable and sweaty (like a hot, humid day) and he worried that he would look like a fool if open meetings occurred. He, like others with relatively low self-esteem, got more enjoyment out of a more closed but also more manageable environment, where what was said would be fairly predictable and not take him by surprise. By contrast, those who feel fairly confident of their own ability to react appropriately in nonplanned situations will probably derive more enjoyment from the ebb and flow of a high-disclosure climate.

In terms of comfort with conflict and confrontation, those who find these processes unpleasant would probably experience a high-disclosure climate as stormy, erratic, and prone to sudden shifts in the weather, since both "good" and "bad" items would be raised when people felt they were relevant. What seemed like storms to the low confronters would, on the other hand, feel like brisk autumn weather to those comfortable with confrontation and conflict. These latter people would feel that a low-disclosure climate was sticky and muggy; few bad "storms" occur, since what is dealt with is highly selected and controlled, but an undercurrent of sluggishness effectively stifles feelings of joy and verve.

In low-disclosure climates, the slow, sticky times may be followed by periods of explosive storms or blowups, when issues that have been systematically ignored become unavoidable and burst to the surface. Recently, many universities have experienced this phenomenon, not a particularly pleasant occurrence for either low- or high-conflict types. In low-disclosure organizations members can often feel changes in pressure as suppressed issues become more critical, almost as if they had barometers to detect rises and falls in tension.

There is not much research to support our final proposition, but our own experience and observations seem to warrant it: over the long-run, a consistently low-disclosure climate is not likely to provide strongly positive pleasure to an organization's members. Like a long run of moderately poor weather, its main feature is the avoidance of highly negative situations (the storms), but it does not provide high positive experience either. By contrast, a high-disclosure climate may have negative periods, highs and lows, and changeable conditions, but on the average people will feel freer to say and be what they really are, to experiment and to help others to do the same, rather than punishing them for it. This seems to us to provide more possibilities for positive enjoyment for everyone than does a cautious, careful, closed environment where fear of a "wrong move" causes people to calculate before disclosing anything.

Growth

Observation and research point rather consistently to the effectiveness of high-disclosure climates and the relative ineffectiveness of low-disclosure environments in promoting growth. For instance, Sidney Jourard's work, including both *The Transparent Self* and *Disclosing Man to Himself*, indicates that disclosure of self and reactions of others which confirm the essential features of that disclosure are an integral factor in the growth of a healthy personality. Those who are unable to disclose or to accept disclosure from others are not likely to move beyond whatever level of self-awareness they have achieved as a minimum for "getting along" in the world.

At a group level, it is hard for members of a group to learn about the extent of similarities and differences among them if they are restricted to certain regular areas of disclosure. Just as people hide differences when they do not level with one another, so they also miss their common attributes when the range of discussion is restricted. The term "pluralistic ignorance" has been coined for this state: several persons having similar feelings about some event, but each thinking that he or she is the only one who feels that way and therefore it would be foolish to discuss it.

High-disclosure climates tend to generate new data, new ideas, and unpredictable connections which can be inputs to members' growth. By contrast, low-disclosure climates tend toward predictability—much of the communication is actually ritual, with little new information content. Growthful climates require some precipitation (conflict) and some breezes (shared emotionality) if growth is to take place—and that means disclosure. On the other hand, too much disclosure can lead to overly heavy precipitation and gale velocity winds, which threaten the person so much that he or she cannot learn from experience. On the average, it seems better to chance an occasional storm due to high disclosure than to pay the nongrowth consequences of low disclosure.

Finally, low-disclosure climates are actually doubly damaging to individual growth, because they inhibit free and open *responses* to people's behavior or questions. Even if an individual decides to deviate from the norm of a low-disclosure climate and raise a difficult issue, he or she is unlikely to get much response or feedback about the consequences of this action, since the climate says that one should should not give those kinds of reactions to people. If any information is communicated, it is usually long after the actual event occurred. All of this means that individual growth is hampered considerably by a climate of low disclosure, since new learning requires both experimenting with new ideas, actions, feeling, etc., and being able to get back information that is close to the action in both time and place.

NOTES

1. Sidney Jourard, *The Transparent Self* (New York: Van Nostrand-Insight, 1964).
2. See Carl Rogers, *On Becoming a Person* (Boston: Houghton-Mifflin, 1961).
3. Alexander Solzhenitsyn, *The First Circle* (New York: Harper & Row, 1968), p. 339. Reprinted by permission.

4. From Fritz Steele, *The Open Organization: The Impact of Secrecy and Disclosure on People and Organizations* (Reading, Mass.: Addison-Wesley, 1975), p. 69. This is a good reference for those readers who would like to explore further in the areas of disclosure and secrecy generally, as well as the specifics of the Unilateral Relevance Test.

5. C.H. Sisson, "The Civil Service-3: Can Anything Be Done About It?", *The Spectator*, London, 6 March 1971, p. 314. Reprinted by permission.

6. Harold Leavitt, "Some Effects of Certain Communication Patterns on Group Performance," *Journal of Abnormal and Social Psychology* **46** (1951): 38–50.

7. This is similar to the "double bind" situation which has been theorized to be a contributor to the development of schizophrenia. See G. Bateson, D. Jackson, J. Haley, and J. Weakland, "Toward a Theory of Schizophrenia," *Behavioral Science* **1**, no. 4 (1956).

8. Melville Dalton, *Men Who Manage* (New York: Wiley, 1959), p. 227. Copyright © 1959 by John Wiley & Sons, Inc. Reprinted by permission of the publisher.

Chapter 11

Improving the Flow of Information

The desire to improve communications in organizations has probably been the subject of more books, articles, films, and executive-luncheon speeches than any other human organizational problem. Everyone seems to agree that, without communication among people, an organization cannot function. They also agree that they are never doing it as well as they should, that there is room for improvement. There is not very much agreement, however, on how to go about improving communications.

Many people approach it as basically a technical problem: if you have the right techniques, you will communicate well. As may be apparent from Chapter 10, we tend to approach the problem in terms relating more to human motivation and other forces that determine the choice of *whether* to communicate some information to someone else and less to *how* it is done. The basic choice is whether or not to disclose what you know to another person or group.

In this chapter, therefore, we provide a survey of methods that we (and others) have used to increase the *probability* that members of a group or an organization will share with one another the necessary, relevant, or wanted information. We say "probability" because we believe that single events are not as critical as the longer-term pattern of what is being shared, when, and to whom. It is this disclosure pattern that we change in order to improve an organization's effectiveness, adaptability, and climate.

159

We deal with four broad categories of change targets:

Content: Expanding the range of allowable topic areas;

Sending skills: Enhancing peoples' abilities to communicate information;

Receiving skills: Enhancing peoples' abilities to receive messages effectively;

Context: Influencing the settings and other nonperson factors that help to determine the patterns of disclosure in a system.

CONTENT

As discussed in the previous chapter, a number of the blocks to disclosure (and therefore to a satisfying and invigorating climate) are caused by limitations placed on particular topic areas, "rules of the game" about which topic areas are acceptable or unacceptable, relevant or irrelevant, healthy or unhealthy. There are also rules about who can receive which topics and in which situations. When we are trying to stimulate a freer, more spontaneous (or unpredictable) flow of information shaped by actual needs and events rather than by preprogrammed rules, we try to reduce the degree to which restrictions are placed on various topics. The following activities are a sampling of some of the means we have used to these ends.

Decreasing the Number of Taboo Areas

One of our most frequent change goals is to try to decrease the number of taboos or unspeakable topics that exist in the system, thereby creating both a freer climate and better opportunities for people to deal with problems in the taboo areas. Our basic methodology is to have a group conduct a taboo census, with the same main elements as the norm census described in Chapter 5. (Taboos are essentially a special class of norms which control verbal behavior.) We will not repeat all the steps here, but the basic parts are: (a) describe the main taboos operating in your system (topics that cannot be discussed at all); (b) describe the conditional taboos (rules about who can say what to whom in which situations); (c) discuss examples of the costs of systematic taboos and identify which ones are blocking the group the most; and (d) set some specific change goals for which taboo areas should be loosened or eliminated altogether.

In getting a taboo census started, you face the same problem as in the supernorms dilemma: there usually is a taboo against discussing the fact that there are taboos operating! The person who raises the problem runs some risk of being branded as disloyal, immature, inconsiderate, or whatever by the rest of the group. Getting started therefore generally calls for (a) a first move by someone with such a solid status that he or she is running a small risk, (b) a first move by someone who is willing to take a larger risk, or (c) the initiation or support of someone outside the group (such as a consultant) who has both credibility and enough independence not to feel threatened by speaking the unspeakable in the group.

Although an outsider can help to start a taboo census, the group members themselves must be involved in all the steps or they will not really commit themselves to much experimentation or change. They will tend to write off the issues raised by the outsider as unsuitable topics (as one executive put it) "raised by someone who couldn't really know better because he's not one of us."

Survey Feedback:
Practicing the Generation of Shared Data

One of the most extensively developed technologies in the applied behavioral sciences is that of using survey research techniques to generate data about the attitudes, opinions, perceptions, and values held by members of groups and organizations.[1] This process has a fairly general acceptance in many organizations today. A survey is taken by questionnaire or other means; the data are summarized and interpreted in some manner; there is some kind of feedback of the results of the data collection agents to some parts of the organization, usually at least to the executive(s) that authorized the survey; some problem areas are identified; and some sort of action plans are generated, often including a follow-up survey to check progress at some point in the future.

In our own use of survey data, we generally communicate the data patterns to all (including the managers) who provided the basic responses, for we feel that one of the biggest payoffs from surveys comes from the pattern they help establish, not just from the identification of specific problems. This pattern is the increased discussion of issues, problems, and possibilities by all levels of the system. The matter-of-fact feeding back of summaries of identified problems, if it includes more than the top managers, can help everyone feel more comfortable with topics that have been scary or taboo (or both). The structured process helps legitimize the sharing of information about problems and makes those who do it less vulnerable to charges of disloyalty, backstabbing, or powerhunger; the formal process therefore reduces the personal cost of breaking the taboos. It also tends to increase peoples' expectations that some concrete improvements will come out of the survey⟶feedback⟶planning ⟶action⟶evaluation cycle.

We do not have the space to deal with specific survey research methods here. Those interested in applying them in their organizations should contact a consultant with a reputation for successfully combining survey methods with action planning.

At the group level, simpler methods can often stimulate improved information flow. One technique is for group members to fill out a 5–10 item questionnaire at the end of group meetings, describing how effectively they thought they functioned as a group. The results may not go down in the annals of elegant research studies, but the repetition of the process helps people to be more comfortable with disclosing to one another their true perceptions of the group's processes.

Quick Feedback about Disclosure Choices

With a group that has become relatively committed to looking at its own communications patterns, it is possible to take more direct approaches. One of these is a simple (in design, not impact) exercise called, "What Did We *Not* Say Today?" At the close of a meeting (or even a two-person interchange), each member tries to write down most of the things he or she thought about saying but chose not to say during the course of the event. One person collects these and the process is repeated for several meetings. Then the same person puts all of the lists together and categorizes the topics. Another meeting is held for the purpose of examining the trends and patterns of what people are regularly not saying to one another. The topics are listed on newsprint by category (with the date of the item noted beside it to help in spotting possible changes over time) and the group tries to associate the unspoken data with the processes and results of the meetings. The goal is to show the group both unconscious patterns of low disclosure and the unrecognized, unintended consequences of these patterns.

Because this exercise tends to make people nervous, it is generally a slow starter. Our experience has been, however, that each attempt to compile the "unspokens" list is easier and the overall data turn out to be quite rich and useful.

Reducing Fears of the Unknown

Another exercise we have used with task groups that have had some experience with looking at their own process is called, "Catastrophe, Anyone?" Each member of the group writes an anonymous list of the sensitive topics that they fear others (not themselves) would be too embarrassed to discuss in the presence of most of the group members. These lists are summarized on newsprint and displayed for all to see, usually by a consultant helping with the exercise.

The group is asked to rank these topics (particularly repeating ones) according to the payoff to the group if the topic could become an area for free disclosure and discussion. The four or five highest payoff items are then selected for closer examination. People are asked to share their predictions about what would happen if these topics were discussed. What "catastrophes" are being averted by staying away from these areas? They are also asked to list some of the assumptions that lie behind these predictions. For example, a prediction of embarrassment for someone is often founded on the assumption that "everyone expects everyone else to do everything perfectly: no one ever makes mistakes."

We (the consultant, or whoever is leading the process) then ask the group to consider several questions: (a) Are these predictions actually likely to happen in this group? (b) Are the assumptions that lie behind the predictions true for us? (c) Should they be true? (d) Do we want them to remain, or should we change some of our patterns?

This exercise generally produces three results. It helps to identify predictions and assumptions that are patently false, where in fact nothing negative would happen if a particular topic were raised. It helps to identify predictions and assumptions that are presently true but not satisfactory. And it provides a structured situation in which to practice talking about content areas that are usually avoided.

Our hope is that the impact of this and the other activities just described will be to expand the range of topics about which people will share information, and to do it for a variety of organizational situations, not just for sessions formally labelled as communication or disclosure exercises.

IMPROVING SENDING SKILLS

Another general change strategy is to improve peoples' ability to share information with one another. One side of this ability is competence at sending messages: communicating information so that it has a high probability of being accurately received by the sender. Since so much literature has been produced over the past fifty years on the process of communicating[2], we will not attempt to list the many training devices here. We would, however, like to share several points relating to how one thinks about the process of developing better sending skills.

The sending problem has two main facets: (a) What is my motivation? Do I really *want* to share information with others? What threats does this raise for me and am I willing to take the risk? (b) How effective is my behavior when I decide that I do want to communicate something to someone? On the average, can I send the message that I intend to send?

Motivation

People tend to have personal preferences or styles related to how much information they want to share with others. Basic trust is a factor here, as are values and definitions of the world and its threats.³ There is a range of learning methodologies that can help people learn more about their own disclosure patterns and how they can become more able to share information without feeling vulnerable.

At the high-intensity end of the scale would be such depth experiences as psychotherapy, psychiatric counseling, or Gestalt therapy. These processes are useful for those who feel so blocked or conflicted emotionally that they cannot engage in the kinds of information sharing they rationally believe are required in their situations.⁴ In the middle of the scale are group-training experiences, such as T-groups, encounter groups, Erhard Seminar Training, and the like, which provide short but intense opportunities to experiment in human communications. Finally, you can attempt to examine your disclosure motivation by looking at choices you make in your own live work settings. This, of course, is potentially less intensive than therapy or encounter experiences, but has the added risk of requiring the help of people with whom you will usually continue to work. Therapy and group training permit experimentation in a setting where mistakes will generally not have a high lasting cost.

Behavior

Even assuming that you want to communicate, how effective you are at doing it remains an open question. This is often a hard determination to make by oneself, since most people believe they are good at communicating with others (even though other people might not be very effective at getting the message).

Because of the difficulty in accurately assessing one's own level of skill in certain areas, we do not put much faith in change methods (like "how-to" books or training lectures) which attempt to tell people the "rules" about the right ways to communicate. These methods skip the crucial step: recognizing and owning up to one's room for growth in the communication process. We therefore favor experience-based methods, including encounter groups, T-groups, skill-training exercises, and on-the-job (or in-the-relationship) feedback from someone who is willing to tell you how they perceive you communicating.

For example, we recently worked on a communication problem with a company's middle-management team. We presented a few theoretical concepts, such as taboos and the costs and gains of low disclosure, but the primary emphasis was on actually doing things—on experimenting with new behaviors in the communications process. In particular, we had them practice *sharpening* their messages to one another during problem-solving sessions. Each person tried to say exactly what he wanted to communicate to another person and to specify exactly for whom the message was intended. The point was not that they always should behave this way in their meetings; it was to have them briefly experiment with another mode so that they could *experience the difference* between straight messages and the overloaded, mixed combinations they usually sent while thinking they were being perfectly clear.

IMPROVING RECEIVING SKILLS

A great deal has also been written about the problems associated with the other side of the communication process: how to receive information in an accurate, undistorted manner. Again, we will not present detailed training activities, but will briefly describe three specific skills whose enhancement would be a goal of such training. They are focused listening, reflecting, and screening.

Focused Listening

Many people involved in the study of psychology and human relations consider listening to be a fundamental requirement of interpersonal competence. There is one aspect of listening that we feel has not been emphasized as much as it should be: the ability to focus on the main point or theme of what the other person is saying and not be distracted by side issues or other less-important messages. People very often do just the opposite: they respond to a word or phrase that constitutes only a small part of what the other person is saying (so the listener can say, if challenged, that he *was* being responsive.) The word or phrase is usually related, at least tangentially, to something the *receiver* wanted to say anyway. For example, "Oh yes, speaking of dogs, I saw a golden retriever today," is not a particularly helpful response from a boss whose subordinate has just complained that he is being worked to death like an old dog.

In other words, we often don't hear the main theme because it serves our interests not to hear it. This is not illegal or immoral, but as a pattern it should not be confused with free, effective information flow. When receivers respond to tangential points, it is very difficult to have a conversation that is likely to lead somewhere. Each person is too busy thinking of ways to respond to what they wished the other person had said.

Focusing on the main theme can be practiced in many regular situations: one-to-one conversations, group meetings, political conferences, watching television (especially talk shows where host and guest often miss each other completely), and so on. Continually ask yourself: What is the *essence* of what they are saying right now—what is the main point? If you work at asking and answering that question, the responsiveness tends to follow rather easily as your awareness improves.

Reflection

By reflecting, we mean the regular reflecting back to the sender of what you think are the main points of the message, so that the communication is a two-way process. Reflecting is worth cultivating as a habit, since it keeps the information-exchange process from being a closed system. When receivers do *not* test their perceptions through reflection, each person tends to think they are doing a good job of sending and receiving, no matter what the actual level of effectiveness may be. Consequently, there is very little likelihood that they can correct their process if it is, in fact, not going well.

Screening for Relevance

Since a climate of *totally* open disclosure would be as oppressive (or more so) than one where no one disclosed anything, selectivity about what one discloses is essential. On the sender's side, discretion can be exercised by unilaterally deciding what the other person needs to know (the aforementioned

Unilateral Relevance Test[5]), or by discussing with the other person (or the group) whether a particular piece of information is desired/useful/relevant (called the Joint Relevance Test).

The receiver, on the other hand, must be willing and able to respond to questions or tests for relevance without becoming muddled or locked in to automatic responses. This need is particularly acute at the level of group functioning. Most groups are not very good at screening trial balloons for relevance. They either reject them out of hand as being the act of a "blocker who is slowing our progress" or they automatically talk about whatever is thrown out for testing, thus putting a great burden on the tester to be right in his or her judgments about relevance. We therefore strongly recommend that both individuals and groups develop the habits of (a) asking the question, Is what the other person is saying now relevant to what I (we) need or want to know? and (b) providing some response (positive or negative) about the relevance, so that the receiver has a hand in controlling the quality of the communicative process. The trick here is to be able to evaluate the relevance of a topic without simultaneously evaluating the fact that the person raised it at all.

In sum, we use two criteria to judge the effectiveness of a receiver's behavior: (1) in the specific instance, has it helped to ensure the *accuracy* of the communication? and (2) has it helped to encourage the *continuation of an effective process* in the future? It is not very beneficial to "get something straight" with a sender if your manner of doing so discourages the person from ever telling you anything of importance again.

THE CONTEXT OF DISCLOSURE

The fourth main target area for improving the climate for disclosure is the context in which communications occur. By "context" we mean both physical and social settings: the physical spaces in which people operate; the distances and barriers they must cross; the presence or absence of electronic media to speed communications; the norms about disclosure which form policies about who can disclose what and to whom; and so on.

Since we dealt with the impact and change of physical settings in Chapters 8 and 9, we focus here on a few change strategies related to the social context of disclosure. These include policy changes, structural changes, and power tactics.[6]

Policy Changes

If an organization's managers really want to improve the disclosure climate in their system, they have tools at their disposal for helping to make it happen. They can change the general thrust of policies that require people to be unnecessarily secretive by utilizing the system's reward structures—i.e., if disclosure were rewarded (with positive performance reviews, salary boosts, promotional opportunities, or praise from boss, peers, and subordinates), it would be more likely to occur in the future. At present, many organizations reward just the opposite: secrecy and tight control of all kinds of innocuous information.

In one organization, for example, new statements about the positive value of greater openness were written into the corporate-philosophy statement. In addition, concrete behavioral indicators of this openness (e.g., keeping subordinates informed, sharing timely data with colleagues, etc.) were identified and included in measures of managerial job performance. Over a period of a year and a half, there was a noticeable increase in the amount of information sharing which occurred in the system. This did not happen in a vacuum, however. The policy changes were supported by training sessions on the dynamics of low and high disclosure and on some of the skills described earlier in this chapter.

Structural Changes

As far as communicating is concerned, the "feel" of a place is often influenced by the shape of the structure and your position in it. One of the earliest findings in research on groups was that people felt more or less powerful/included/satisfied, depending on the structure of the group and their location (e.g., central or pheripheral) in it; and a major factor in this effect was whether they had regular access to information about what was going on during the group's task work.[7]

Those who influence structures in the system should periodically perform a diagnostic check to determine who feels they are operating in an information vacuum. They should then ask whether this vacuum is a necessary function of the tasks being performed or the result of a particular structure (or position), perhaps one of several possible ways the work could be organized. The work of behavioral scientists interested in "socio-technical systems" would help you to examine how these structural choices have been made and how they could potentially be made differently.[8]

Power Tactics

Although we have not discussed the relationship between disclosure and power balances in an organization, power dynamics strongly affect the likelihood of change. People often share or withhold information based on their perception of which action is likely to enhance or maintain their own personal (or group) power base. Disclosure thus can be used as a power tactic, often very effectively.

Unfortunately, the reverse influence process is not practiced as often — that is, using various other power tactics as a means of improving the flow of information. Many organization members squander their most potent influence resources: their own energy, time, and information. They give these to people whom they know are withholding selected information from them, as if the two actions had nothing to do with each other. Our suggestion is for people to be direct about using bargaining tactics to improve the flow of information they receive. One way to accomplish this is to engage in periodic "role negotiation" sessions (designed by Roger Harrison), where each person specifies what they expect to get and will give to the other person, with agreement on what happens if either of them breaches the contract.[9]

Obviously, many other power tactics could be used to increase the level of disclosure in a system. Other examples would be collective action, where a group of people join in withholding their services until more information is available; innundating others with unselected information until a new bargain can be struck; and carefully documenting particular cases where a lack of disclosure resulted in very negative consequences for a group or for the organization as a whole.[10]

We have also found that one's influence in this area can be used more effectively if realistic goals are set. For example, a demand that a company publish and distribute to every employee all data that it formerly held secret has a number of forces working against it, not the least of which is the sheer massiveness of the task compared with the arguable benefits and risks. A more realistic goal would be to have the secrecy policy changed to an availability policy, with information available to those who request it and a master catalogue of types of existing information and how one can obtain them also available. The latter is especially important—theoretical availability of data is useless if people don't know of the data's existence or how to get access to it.

Another power tactic that is becoming more widely used in the United States is to try to focus outside environmental forces on the people whose behavior you are trying to alter. Many sources of influence have been used for this end: customer boycotts; governmental regulation, such as the Truth in Advertising laws or the Freedom of Information Act, which was passed to enhance disclosure within the various federal bureaucracies themselves; mass stockholder actions; and general public opinion (when it can be sufficiently focused). System members generally tend to feel it is disloyal, immature, destructive, or whatever, to use these kinds of influence modes to effect changes in their organization. And those at the top of the system will, of course, encourage them to feel exactly that way, since it keeps the members from bringing to bear the full range of possible influence startegies available to them. Our recommendation is simply that people should think more about what they want to accomplish and how they could help that to happen and less about what a "nice person" (as defined by those opposed to the change) would do.

SUMMARY

This chapter has been concerned with improving climate through implementing two types of change in the communication process:

- Shorter-term changes, such as increasing the availability of specific areas of information in particular situations
- Longer-term changes in the pattern of disclosure
  —diagnosing and altering taboos

— changing who can get what information

— helping the free-disclosure process to become insti-
tutionalized, so that it feels natural and not forced

— creating structural supports and removing structural
blocks, so that you are changing aspects of the formal system as well as how people behave face-to-face.

The change activities we have discussed have been aimed
at both reducing the forces that restrain disclosure and
increasing the forces that encourage disclosure. If you are interested in further exploring this area and would like to do something concrete, we suggest you see Part V of Steele's *Open
Organization* (see footnote 5). This book contains a number of
other semiclassic change activities, such as "Airing the Dirty
Linen and Liking It," "Priming the Pump (Try It, You'll Like
It. . .)," and "No More Mr. Nice Guy."

NOTES

1. The work of the Survey Research Center at the University of
    Michigan has led the way in this development. For examples of
    the use of survey information to promote organizational improve-
    ment, see S. Seashore and D. Bowers, *Changing the Structure and
    Functioning of an Organization* (Ann Arbor: Institute for Social Re-
    search, 1963); and R.S. Jenks, "An Action-Research Approach to
    Organizational Change," in W. Burke and H. Hornstein, eds., *The
    Social Technology of Organization Development* (Fairfax, Va.:
    NTL Learning Resources Corp., 1972).

2. The literature in management abounds with advice and rules on
    how to be a good communicator—focusing mostly on the techni-
    cal problems, as we mentioned earlier.

3. For a very nice discussion of these individual differences and the
    factors that cause them, see S. Jourard, *The Transparent Self* (New
    York: Van Nostrand (Insight), 1964).

4. We know that some percentage of the people who read this book
    could profit very much from this kind of therapeutic experience,
    but there is no way to estimate what the percentage is or who the
    specific people are. You have to be willing to be at least honest
    enough with yourself to say that you would like to try something
    in this area, even though it may be scary or uncomfortable.

5. From Fritz Steele, *The Open Organization* (Reading, Mass:
    Addison-Wesley, 1975).

6. Parts of this discussion are drawn from *The Open Organization* (see footnote 5), Chapter 19.

7. See H. Leavitt, "Some Effects of Certain Communication Patterns on Group Performance," in *Journal of Abnormal and Social Psychology* **46** (1951): 38–50.

8. For an introduction, see the classic book by the Tavistock Socio-Technical Group, E. Trist, G. Higgin, H. Murray, and A. Pollack, *Organizational Choice* (London: Tavistock Publications, 1963).

9. See R. Harrison, "Role Negotiation: A Tough-Minded Approach to Team Development," in W. Bennis, E. Schein, D. Berlew, and F. Steele, eds., *Interpersonal Dynamics*, 3d ed. (Homewood, Illinois: Dorsey Press, 1973).

10. For other suggestions, see Barry Oshry, "Notes on Power," 1974, produced by Power & Systems Training, Inc., Box 388, Prudential Station, Boston, Mass. 02199.

Chapter 12

Strategies for Starting and Implementing Change

Throughout this book the discussion has alternated among several general themes: basic concepts of climate, examples of special climates, and improving the effects of climate on people and organizations. Ideas and concepts have been presented with the purpose not only of explaining what climate is about, but also of sensitizing people to become better able to perceive the climates in which they work and which they help to create for other people.

It is not enough, of course, simply to say that readers should now have a better understanding of organization climate and therefore be able to change it as they wish. The process used to change the climate is itself both a cause and a reflection of the climate. Therefore, it is important that the strategy employed to initiate climate change be consistent with the desired outcome of the change. For example, changes toward greater participation in decision making as a step toward increasing the distribution of energy in a system should generally not be initiated by an edict from those at the top! If the organization is too centralized with regard to disclosure and decision making, much of the supportive energy for change must exist outside the central group if the change is to succeed.

DESCRIPTION

In order to develop a strategy for starting and implementing climate change in a system, several steps must be completed (roughly) in sequence. The first step is to describe the climate as it currently exists. Some of the techniques for accomplishing this step have been outlined in some detail in Chapters 3 (the section on "Sensing Your Climate"), 4, and 5 (particularly the Norm Census). Other techniques are outlined below.

Questionnaire Surveys

One means for describing the climate of a system is to conduct a relatively formal opinion survey of the people in the system, asking for their views of the organization or the group in regard to specific dimensions. Litwin and Stringer[1], at the Harvard Business School, have developed a number of dimensions they believe constitute the major variables that make up the climate of an organization, and they have an instrument to measure these. The dimensions are:

1. Structure (clarity, degree)
2. Responsibility (demands on people; individual vs. group)
3. Rewards (what kinds, amounts)
4. Risk (from caution to risk taking)
5. Warmth (feeling of closeness or distance from one another)
6. Support (felt from superiors and peers)
7. Standards (the degree of "demandingness" of the system)
8. Conflict (the degree of open confrontation—how conflict is handled)
9. Identity (the extent to which people identify with the group vs. the organization)

Another questionnaire approach which is less elaborate than formal surveys is for a group to develop its own series of questions describing important features of its climate, and have members respond to this periodically. One group developed six simple items on seven-point scales such as, "I feel involved in what we are doing," "We are working effectively as a group," and so on. They filled these out after each meeting (sometimes called a Post Meeting Reaction sheet, or PMR) so that they had a running record (plotted on wall charts) of their climate, similar to charts used for sales and production figures. Another group did the same thing, except that they mailed all their sheets each time to an outside consultant who would then call a special process meeting to deal with climate problems when the ratings went outside certain specified limits. In essence, they were trying to operate a quality-control process on their human processes as well as on their business and technical processes.

In a similar vein, but on a more specific one-shot basis, Richard Beckhard[2] has developed what he calls "The Confrontation Meeting." He, as a consultant, gathers data on how members perceive a system, its climate, and its main problems, using both written comments and interviews. He does not rely on these data as the "diagnosis," however, nor is this collection process an elaborate affair stretching over weeks and months. He completes it in a matter of days, then designs a feedback session where he describes what *he* sees from his data collection and also works with those present to (a) test whether his views fit with the members' descriptions of their system; and (b) specify some of the *causes* of the state of the system. His assumption is a good one: that a survey of members' views is only as good as their initial understanding and awareness of organizational processes. Although he starts with member perceptions, the confrontation meeting itself serves an integral function in stimulating *new* ways of looking at what happens to people and their effectiveness in that climate.

The Weather Metaphor

The necessity of developing richer ways of perceiving in order to describe organization climate is the most basic reason for our use of the extended metaphor of organizational "weather." Hopefully, thinking in these terms will help people develop new ways of perceiving what they do and what happens to them, thereby making them better diagnosticians about the climate of their organizations. Another means for describing organization or group climate is to further pursue the physical-weather metaphor, asking yourself and others to free associate around the following kinds of questions:

- How much do I need to wear foul-weather gear here?
- How changeable is the weather and what regular warning signs occur before it changes?
- How comfortable is it for me here? For other people with different styles or roles?

- Who are the weather forecasters that we rely on to predict what things will be like here?
- Are there different zones within the organization that have very different climates? Who tends to end up in each of these zones?
- When there are storms in this system, are they fast moving or slow moving?
- Who can *do* something about the weather here as well as talk about it?
- Which people and what kinds of ideas can grow in this climate, and which die out?
- Who are the sources of energy in this system? Where are they located?
- Is there enough breeze (emotional expressiveness) in this system?
- Is there enough precipitation (conflict and challenge) in the system for people to grow?

These kinds of questions can provide a good framework for understanding the "feel" of the system for those who are in it.

The Physical Setting

Still another means of obtaining data about the climate of a system is to move around in that system and observe the physical settings and how people use them. This kind of observation can provide one with another view of what it feels like to be in a particular organization or group—one that is sometimes harder to cover up than the words people use to describe their work places in social-system terms.

Many guidelines for looking at the physical setting for cues about climate were discussed in Chapters 8 and 9. To recap briefly, the setting as a reflection of climate can be understood by asking questions such as:

- Where do people tend to go in this space when they have free moments?
- What kinds of things have people done to their places to re-flect themselves as persons? (If there are few signs of this kind of influence, people may feel transient in this system.)

- What do arrangements, locations, furniture, etc. say about relative status or power in this system?
- Do the work areas look as if the people in them *care* about the areas (and also about themselves)?
- Do the arrangements of furniture, moveable walls, etc. say anything about how people want to relate to one another—close/distant, visible/hidden, free movement/controlled movement, and so on?
- Do people use their settings in patterns that suggest they *like* spending time here? Do they choose to be here when they have an option?
- What do facilities and layouts suggest about the norms of the system, and about how loose or constraining the whole normative system feels to members?

Similar questions can be asked when thinking about the physical setting as a *cause* of a particular climate. For example:

- What kind of mood (institutional sameness, vitality, work orientation, etc.) are the arrangements and colors likely to foster here?
- Who can get together easily, given this arrangement, and can people develop connections with one another in this setting?
- How elaborate are the rules about how the spaces and facilities can be used? To what extent do these rules present a "pressing down" climate, where people are visibly reminded of how little freedom of expression they have?
- What do patterns set up by traffic (foot and vehicle), noise, lighting, etc. provide as a climate for existing or growing? Do they make it difficult to experiment, concentrate, demonstrate, and so on?

Sabbaticals

A valuable way to gain new awareness of your own organization climate is to venture "behind the scenes" in other organizations to get a feel for the kinds of climates that have evolved there. Many of us have the same problem fish have with water—our climate is so much a regular part of life that it is difficult to be aware of it, and it is especially difficult to be aware of our climate as an *alternative* rather than as a *given*.

A system that places some value on understanding and improving its own climate can benefit from providing visits or sabbaticals to its members to support their learning about other organizations, so that they can more clearly see their own. A basically closed organization would not want to follow a strategy of this sort, however, since people may be more dissatisfied once they are exposed to other possibilities. The issue, of course, is whether the awareness of climate alternatives is looked upon as a *threat* (raising dissatisfaction) or as a *resource* (new awareness, with dissatisfaction being used as a source of energy and information for change and improvement). Our view is that, in the long run, systems are more likely to provide productive and satisfying environments if they are willing to develop an understanding of what they have chosen as a climate and how this differs from the climates in other organizations. In addition, sabbaticals can have very beneficial payoffs not only in terms of the person's increased understanding of his or her own organization's climate, but also for the rejuvenation of the person individually.[3]

New Observers

One final means of describing climate will be mentioned briefly, mainly because it is seldom used (often for the reasons of threat mentioned above). This means is the resource that a new member represents. As a recent arrival from another culture, a new member is in a position to articulate what it feels like to be in your climate as compared with his or her previous cultures or climates. Although the climates may be quite similar, the odds are that there will be some significant differences in the mood and feel of the places, as well as in the kinds of protective "clothing" that are felt to be needed in each.

At the point when the new observer has been with the system long enough to have the "feel" of it, yet not so long that he or she has forgotton other climates, the new person could be a valuable source of diagnostic data about system climate. Yet in most groups this resource is not used and, in fact, is avoided. Experiences in this early period are designed to get the newcomer "on board," to "teach him the ropes"—in other words, to make the newcomer "one of us" just as fast as possible. This socialization process is undoubtedly partly motivated by the wish to make the newcomer a productive and accepted member of the group; but it may also be spurred by the fear of an open examination of climate. This rapid assimilation is often further accelerated by the new person himself. When one is just entering a new group or organization, anxiety or concern about group acceptance is probably at its highest level. If the group sends out any cues indicating it would be angry if the newcomer told members how it really felt to be in the group and what he or she observes about the way they relate to one another, the new person is likely to consider the risk of being kept out as greater than the gain of sharing observations. This suggests that the major burden for making the new member a diagnostic resource should fall on the existing group. In order to encourage the process, the group needs to communicate to the new person that (a) they value and can handle his or her observations about the climate—they actively want to know what it feels like for the person; and (b) there will not be recriminations if the newcomer shares observations with them. If both of these messages are believed by the group and communicated to the new member, he or she can indeed be a valuable source of input in describing the group's climate.

DIAGNOSIS

The second major step after describing one's climate is to make a diagnosis based on the information in the description. Some diagnostic "windows" were presented in Chapter 3 (the section on "Diagnosing What's Wrong") and further diagnostic material is presented in Chapter 5 (the section on "Assessing the Consequences of the Norm System"). A basic consideration for any particular diagnostic technique is the set of underlying assumptions made about the nature of a "good" climate.

In our choice of the four weather dimensions, we have implied a set of assumptions about what constitutes a good climate. We assume that one end of each of these four dimensions promotes a better climate than the other end, almost independent of the kind of organization being considered. In general, we believe that changes in the "favorable" direction along any one of the four dimensions or a combination of them will lead to a better climate. However, the same kind of climate can have beneficial effects in one kind of system and damaging effects in another. The kind of climate that makes a healthy research organization may differ in some important ways from the kind of climate required to make a healthy manufacturing organization. Although the similarities between good climates in different types of organizations exceed the differences, the possibility of differences must be kept in mind.

Some frame of reference is essential for making an accurate diagnosis. To use the weather analogy, one could *describe* a snowstorm and draw very *different diagnostic conclusions* about the snowstorm's positive value, depending on where it occurred—in, for example, Sun Valley, Idaho versus Tucson, Arizona. The event is the same, but the diagnostic frame of reference is different. Therefore, to make a good diagnosis about an organization's climate, some things must be known (and articulated) about what would be an ideal climate for the system. Then descriptive information concerning the current climate can be evaluated against the characteristics of the ideal climate, and a diagnosis can be formulated.

The size of the gap between the actual climate and the ideal is one measure of the health of the organization. Before developing methods to close the gap, a further diagnostic step is necessary: an analysis of the discrepancy (if any) between what is *needed* and what is *possible*. Clearly, if the changes needed to move toward a more ideal climate are impossible to achieve, then trying to accomplish them is a useless activity.

This recommendation may sound more pessimistic than intended, but it is important to recognize that you will be less frustrated if you try to change elements of the climate that you have at least some chance of influencing. The notion of sequence becomes very relevant in this kind of diagnosis. If you work on more changeable areas first, your effects can improve the probability that other (previously uninfluenceable) dimensions can now be affected. An obvious example was our earlier recommendation that the sequence for norms change requires that you first alter the norm against talking openly about norms.

One way to determine what changes are feasible is to assess the sources of support for any planned change. In general, the more support there is, the more possible it is to implement the change. Support may come from outside the organization as well as from within. Outside influences include legislation and

"... But has it actually helped production-wise?"

government regulation (for example, OSHA and EEO)[4] and the increasing pressure on corporations in the area of social responsibility, pressure that is likely to increase with the attention being paid to the "quality of work life" issue. These and other external pressures can be powerful sources of support for proposed internal changes and can be used to stimulate the momentum needed to move toward a more ideal climate.

Timing can be an important source of support for change and a determinant of its success. If a diagnosis and recommendations for change are initiated at the right time ("when things are ripe for change"), the fact that the timing is good can be an impetus for action. If the very same diagnosis and recommendations are sprung at the wrong time, such as during a very bad economic period when people are concerned about the very survival of the organization, the likelihood of failure is dramatically increased.

STRATEGIES FOR ACTION

The third step toward changing climate is the development of various strategies for action. The particular strategy developed will depend on what is possible and who is initiating the change. Table 12.1 presents some typical target factors for changing the four climate dimensions used throughout this book. Strategies for action will differ depending on which target area is being focused on as well. Of the three aspects influencing strategy development, the most important is who is attempting to stimulate the change. We have discriminated three simple categories of initiator: those with high power in the system, those with medium power, and those with low power.

High-Power People

Those with high system power have a wide choice of strategies for introducing change, depending on how much they wish to utilize their power in accomplishing the change. The more centralized the planning for the change is, the more difficult it will be to obtain from others support for and commitment to the change. Our experience indicates that attempts to change

Table 12.1
Targets for Changing Climate Dimensions

Target Areas	Climate Dimensions			
	Energy	Distribution	Pleasure	Growth
Reward systems	X	X	X	X
Norms	X	X	X	X
Disclosure patterns	X			X
Goals and Goal-Setting processes		X		
Managerial style		X	X	X
Decision-making processes	X	X	X	X
Organizational excitement	X		X	
Career development systems/patterns	X			X
Physical structures		X	X	
Problem-solving skills		X		
Intergroup relations		X	X	
Formal policies	X		X	
Uses of humor			X	

Note: These 13 target areas are shown in a descending order of impact (from *our* point of view) on organization climate. The particular climate dimensions that each of them is most likely to affect are marked with X's, again from our point of view.

climate which emanate from high-power people, without the involvement of those affected, tend to encounter a great deal of resistance. In one case, an executive became interested in open-office planning and decided to institute such a scheme "to create a more open climate" in a new building he was planning. The new layout was effectively sabotaged by creative uses of filing cabinets and makeshift walls. Certainly he had the formal power to make the initial change in the physical setting by himself, but had he involved some of those to be affected by his decision prior to making it, he would probably have had a smaller backlash of resistance to the idea. Ironically, he was closed to the inputs of others while trying to create a more open climate.

If high-power people do allow others in the system to influence the direction and/or degree of change, they may not end up with what they want, but are likely to have generated greater commitment to the change(s).

Medium-Power People

This term probably describes the vast majority of readers of this book. Since few of you are in positions of high power, you must base any strategies for change on your anticipated sources of support. Attention to timing as an integral part of your change strategy is important as well. Potential sources of support include those with more power and those with less power, and in both cases is dependent on their trust and confidence in you. The development of a strategy for change must be a communicative and collaborative process in which you are seen as working in the overall best interests of the organization. Anything short of that will cause an erosion in your power base.

Another, more risky way of thinking about your options for inducing change is to consider the special features of your position as a "middle" power holder. While this position certainly has many constraints built into it, it also carries potential leverage for inducing climate change. The leverage comes from the fact that almost everyone wants something from you — something that you could consider withholding, in certain situations, until some new behavior was exhibited by the person who wanted you to "play ball."

Most middle-power people tend not to use this bargaining power, either because of the external threat to one's organizational career or because of the internal threat of guilt, of not feeling like a "good person" if one withholds something that has been automatically given away in the past (information, assistance, time, or whatever). We believe these threats are exaggerated by the person's view of the world from the middle position and that more leverage for change exists there than is generally used. In fact, both higher-power and lower-power people in the organization usually allow themselves to negotiate more freely than do the middle people. If you are in a middle position, your own standards of how you "should" behave may be severely limiting your ability to induce changes that you feel are good and necessary.

Low-Power People

Those with low power tend to have more options available to them because they have less to lose. Consequently, they may choose to initiate change in a dramatic and highly visible manner (the kamikaze approach). Often, the rather radical and even violent tactics (prisoner revolts, student demonstrations, etc.) employed by low-power people in organizations are the *only* means they have to initiate climate change. People who suddenly *feel* powerless adopt similar change strategies for the same reasons, such as when doctors strike to protest impossibly high malpractice-insurance rates. Any change strategy chosen by a low-power person involves some risk because, depending on the existing fear climate, the very taking of initiative may cause the low-power person to be ejected from the system.

Elements of a Good Strategy

A good strategy for action has several component parts that help to make it successful when implemented:

The right targets are chosen for change. Often, people try to change climate by changing the wrong thing. For example, a change in formal policies is not likely to change the climate very much if the current climate is suffering from problems related to the reward systems or informal norms.

The right people are involved. Who needs to be involved to ensure the proposed change is implemented? Are those people involved and supportive of the change? Do they have a sense of ownership of the change? Do they have the power to make the necessary behavioral or procedural changes?

The right timing is used. Most organizations have a kind of seasonality. Introducing change at the wrong time in the cycle can greatly increase resistance to the change. Changes need to be accepted by those who will be affected by them.

When the targets for change, the people to implement the change, and the time to introduce the change have been chosen, one must decide *how* to introduce the change. Methods range from coercion to collaboration. The greater the degree to which a change is imposed, the greater the need for thorough explanation and justification. Most people do not like continual surprises and will resist a pattern of having things sprung on them. Therefore, it is best to give ample forewarning about the change and its anticipated benefits, so that people have a chance to become accustomed to the idea, perhaps even to anticipate the change eagerly. Even negative changes can be coped with quite well if those affected by them are involved and informed before the fact (for example, the closing of a plant location and the early chance to seek a new job).

A final element of a good change strategy relates to the speed of implementation. Change can be implemented very rapidly (a revolution) or very slowly over time (evolution). Each approach has certain consequences. In general, the more revolutionary the change implementation, the greater the disruption to the system. On the other hand, slow evolutionary change sometimes has a draining effect on systems and their members because the system seems continually in a state of flux. Our own preference is for careful planning (when available time and information allow it), full communication with those involved in and affected by the change, and relatively rapid implementation of the change itself.

In practice you will probably always be using a mixed variety of change strategies: some planned, some unplanned; some fast, some slow; some formal, some informal. We hope the discussions in this book have added to your sense of having choices about what in the climate of your organization you would like to change and how you might go about it. Our purpose has been to make climate more visible, less intuitive, and therefore more available to you as a member of an organization in your efforts to make your work world more pleasurable.

NOTES

1. George H. Litwin and Robert A. Stringer, Jr., *Motivation and Organizational Climate* (Boston: Division of Research, Graduate School of Business Administration, Harvard University, 1968).
2. Richard Beckhard, "The Confrontation Meeting," *Harvard Business Review* **54** (March-April 1967): 149–155.

3. Eli Goldston, "Executive Sabbaticals: About to Take Off?" *Harvard Business Review* **61** (September-October 1973): 57–68.
4. OSHA = Occupational Safety and Health Act. EEO = Equal Employment Opportunity Act.

Additional Reading

The following is an alphabetical listing of books and articles that would be useful for readers who wish to explore the areas of organization climate and climate change in more depth. The numbers in parentheses refer to broad, general categories with which the reading deals, as follows:

1. Overall organization climate as a concept
2. The social environment of organizations
3. People's adaptation to climate
4. Live examples of organizational settings
5. Social norms
6. Changing organization climate
7. Studies of organization climate

(3) Ainsworth, H. "Rigidity, Insecurity and Stress." *Journal of Abnormal and Social Psychology* **56** (1958).

(2,4,6) Argyris, C. *Behind the Front Page.* San Francisco: Jossey-Bass, 1974.

(5) Argyris, C. "Explorations in Interpersonal Competence, I and II. *Journal of Applied Behavioral Science* **1**, nos. 1 and 3 (1965).

(2,5) Argyris, C. *Interpersonal Competence and Organizational Effectiveness.* Homewood, Ill.: Irwin, 1962.

(5,6) Argyris, C. "T-groups for Organizational Effectiveness." *Harvard Business Review* **51** (March–April, 1964).

(2)   Argyris, C. *Understanding Organizational Behavior.* Homewood, Ill.: Dorsey Press, 1961.

(1)   Barker, R. *Ecological Psychology.* Stanford: Stanford University Press, 1968.

(4)   Barker, R., and P. Gump. *Big School Small School.* Stanford: Stanford University Press, 1964.

(3)   Bateson, G., D. Jackson, J. Haley, and J. Weakland. "Toward a Theory of Schizophrenia." *Behavioral Science* 1, no. 4 (1956).

(6)   Beckhard, R. "The Confrontation Meeting." *Harvard Business Review* 54 (March–April, 1967).

(6)   Beckhard, R. *Organization Development: Strategies and Models.* Reading, Mass.: Addison-Wesley, 1969.

(2)   Bennis, W., and P. Slater. *The Temporary Society.* New York: Harper & Row, 1968.

(2,6)   Blake, R., and J. Mouton. *The Managerial Grid.* Houston: Gulf, 1964.

(6)   Burke, W., and H. Hornstein. *The Social Technology of Organization Development.* Fairfax, Va.: N.T.L. Learning Resources Corp., 1972.

(2,3)   Culbert, S. *The Organization Trap.* New York: Basic Books, 1974.

(4)   Dalton, M. *Men Who Manage.* New York: Wiley, 1959.

(7)   Dieterly, D., and B. Schneider. "The Effect of Organizational Environment on Perceived Power and Climate: A Laboratory Study." *Organizational Behavior and Human Performance* 11 (1974): 316.

(1,7)   Forchand, G., and B. Gilmore Von Haller. "Environmental Variation and Studies of Organizational Behavior." *Psychological Bulletin* 62, no. 6 (December 1964): 361–82.

(7)   Friedlander, F., and N. Margulies. "Multiple Impacts of Organizational Climate and Individual Value Systems upon Job Satisfaction." *Personnel Psychology* 22 (1969): 171–83.

(4)   Gerst, M., and R. Moos. "The Social Ecology of University Student Residences." *Journal of Educational Psychology* 63 (1972): 513–22.

(2,4)   Goffman, E. *Asylums: Essays on the Social Situation of Mental Patients and Other Inmates.* Garden City, L.I.: Anchor Books (Doubleday) 1961.

(4,5)   Goffman, E. *Presentation of Self in Everyday Life.* Garden City, L.I.: Anchor Books (Doubleday) 1959.

(1)   Guion, R. "A Note on Organizational Climate." *Organizational Behavior and Human Performance* 9 (1973): 120–25.

(3)   Hall, E. *The Hidden Dimension.* Garden City: Doubleday, 1966.

(1)   Halpin, A., and D. Crofts. *The Organizational Climate of Schools.* Chicago: Midwest Administration Center, University of Chicago, 1963.

(7)   Hellriegel, D., and J. Slocum. "Organizational Climate: Measures, Research and Contingencies." *Academy of Management Journal,* June 1974, pp. 255–80.

(5)   Jackson, J. "Structural Characteristics of Norms." In B. Biddle and E. Thomas, eds., *Role Theory: Concepts and Research.* New York: Wiley, 1966.

(7)   Johannesson, R. "Some Problems in the Measurement of Organizational Climate." *Organizational Behavior and Human Performance* **10** (1973): 118–44.

(7)   Kaczka, E., and R. Kirk. "Managerial Climate Work Groups and Organizational Performance." *Administrative Science Quarterly* **12** (1968): 252–71.

(3)   Kahn, R., D. Wolfe, R. Quinn, and J.D. Snoek. *Organizational Stress.* New York: Wiley, 1964.

(2,3,5) Katz, D., and R. Kahn. *The Social Psychology of Organizations.* New York: Wiley, 1966.

(3)   Kelman, H. "Compliance, Identification, and Internalization." *Journal of Conflict Resolution* **2**, no. 2 (1958).

(7)   Lawler, E., D. Hall, and G. Oldham. "Organizational Climate: Relationship to Organizational Structure Process and Performance." *Organizational Behavior and Human Performance* **11** (1974): 139–55.

(2)   Lawrence, P., and J. Lorsch. *Organization and Environment: Managing Differentiation and Integration.* Boston: Division of Research, Harvard Business School, 1968.

(2,6) Likert, R. *The Human Organization.* New York: McGraw-Hill, 1967.

(1)   Litwin, G., and R. Stringer. *Motivation and Organizational Climate.* Boston: Division of Research, Harvard Business School, 1968.

(5)   Luft, J. *Group Processes.* San Francisco: National Press, 1963.

(4,7) Lyon, H., and J. Invancevich. "An Exploratory Investigation of Organizational Climate and Job Satisfaction in a Hospital." *Academy of Management Journal* **17**, no. 4 (December 1974).

(2)   McGregor, D. *The Human Side of Enterprise.* New York: McGraw-Hill, 1960.

(1,3) Moos, R. *Evaluating Treatment Environments: A Social Ecological Approach.* New York: Wiley, 1974.

(1,4) Payne, R., D. Pheysey, and D. Pugh. "Organization Structure, Organizational Climate, and Group Structure: An Exploratory

Study of Their Relationship in Two British Manufacturing Companies." *Occupation Psychology* **45**, no. 1 (1971): 45–55.

(7)   Pritchard, R., and B. Karasick. "The Effect of Organizational Climate on Managerial Job Performance and Job Satisfaction." *Organizational Behavior and Human Performance* **9** (1973): 126–46.

(6)   Schein, E. *Process Consultation*. Reading, Mass: Addison-Wesley, 1969.

(6)   Seashore, S., and D. Bowers. *Changing the Structure and Functioning of an Organization*. Ann Arbor: Univ. of Michigan, Survey Research Center Monograph #33, 1963.

(6)   Steele, F. *Consulting for Organization Change*. Amherst, Mass.: University of Massachusetts Press, 1974.

(3,6)   Steele, F. *The Open Organization: The Impact of Secrecy and Disclosure on People and Organizations*. Reading, Mass.: Addison-Wesley, 1975.

(6)   Steele, F. *Physical Settings and Organization Development*. Reading, Mass.: Addison-Wesley, 1973.

(3)   Stern, G. *People in Context: Measuring Person-Environment Congruence in Education and Industry*. New York: Wiley, 1970.

(1)   Tagiuri, R., and G. Litwin. *Organizational Climate: Explorations of a Concept*. Boston: Division of Research, Harvard Business School, 1968.

(7)   Waters, L., D. Roach, N. Batlis. "Organizational Climate Dimensions and Job-Related Attitudes." *Personnel Psychology* **27** (1974): 465–76.

(4,5)   Whyte, W. *Street-Corner Society, the Social Structure of an Italian Slum*. Chicago: University of Chicago Press, 1943.

DATE DUE